Hail Columbia!

Hail Columbia!

BY DANA STORY

★

BARRE PUBLISHERS
BARRE MASSACHUSETTS
1970

This book is dedicated to the memory
of Arthur D. Story, Everett B. James
and the men of Essex who created
the *Esperanto, Elsie, Mayflower,*
Puritan, Henry Ford, Columbia
and *Gertrude L. Thebaud*

Acknowledgments

The author wishes to acknowledge a debt of gratitude to Joseph E. Garland of Gloucester, Massachusetts, first for his kindness in writing the introduction to this volume and more especially for his original suggestion of the subject matter. However, even more than these, it was the gentle prodding of Mr. Garland together with many friendly suggestions which encouraged the author to labor through to the book's completion.

Much appreciation is also due to the author's friend, Gordon W. Thomas of Ipswich, Massachusetts, for providing a tremendous amount of background and information on the history of Gloucester's vessels and fishing industry. Next to the *Gloucester Daily Times*, Mr. Thomas's book, *Fast and Able*, was the author's most frequently used reference material.

In addition, the author expresses his great appreciation and thanks to Mr. George G. Story of Ipswich, Mr. John M. Clayton of Rockport, Capt. Lawrence C. McEwen, Capt. Collin S. Powers, the late Capt. Archie MacLeod, Mr. William J. MacInnis, Mr. Everett R. Jodrey, Mr. John J. McLaughlin and the late Mrs. Benjamin Pine, all of Gloucester, for giving literally hours of their time in submitting to interviews and for answering a host of questions, which in many cases must have been trying to the patience. Mr. Clayton has kindly allowed the use of a part of his own research material in the appendix.

Thanks are due also to Mr. Stanley N. Dulong and the late Mr. Charles A. Olsen of Gloucester, Mr. Charles F. Sayle of Nantucket, Mr. George E. Mears of Boston, and Mr. David R. Mulcahy and Mr. John J. Doyle of Essex for their assistance and recollections and for the use of their historical material.

Perhaps one of the most monumental pieces of reference work ever done on a single vessel has been accomplished by Mr. E. Sohier Bosley of Scarsdale, New York, who has spent over sixteen years of his spare time in the preparation of an accurate set of plans and drawings of the schooner *Columbia*. It is the author's good fortune to have a set of these plans, and he has drawn freely upon the information which they provide in the writing of this text. The sail plan appears in the appendix.

Lastly, especial thanks are extended to Mr. Stillman Hilton and the kind ladies of the Sawyer Free Library in Gloucester for their courtesy and friendliness, and to Mr. Philip Chadwick Foster Smith, Mr. Paul Blanchette and Mr. Markham Sexton of the Peabody Museum of Salem.

Dana A. Story
Essex, Massachusetts
November 30, 1969

Contents

Introduction

In my great porch overlooking Gloucester Harbor I have a gallery of photographs of the Fishermen's Races taken by the late Adolph Kupsinel. Centered over the window toward Dog Bar Breakwater and out to sea is a sequence of three that brings every visiting sailor up short.

It's *Columbia*, coming at the camera, then smashing by on a close starboard reach, leaning to it, everything flying but her fore gaff topsail and fisherman, her larboard rail sprayed but not under (just as it should be), whacking out a white whey of wake double the breadth of her beam. High aloft, maybe seventy or eighty feet, the mastheadsmen cling to the crosstrees in the half a gale, and as *Columbia* boils past, the guy at the main hounds leans away out to windard, one-handed, and exuberantly waves his cap at you.

And then she is off and away in a swath of froth, this fantastic, leaping, sexy creature! Wow! I hear the loping smack of her bow, and the hiss of the water and the crack of her counter as an underrunning beam sea gives her a little slap, and the wind thumpet of her canvas. I hear it just as plain. . . . I have a little schooner myself, and I can sense it, the feel of the big ones, if only the echo of them.

That's Gloucester and Piney and old Angus, Marty Welch and Clayt Morrissey and Cooney and Story and the rest all in one, and that's what this superb book is about: the schooner, the Gloucesterman, the most stunning fore and aft sailing rig ever conceived and built by man to cleave the ocean blue in search of the cunning cod—at the peak of its prowess in the 1920s, clipping along on the very edge of extinction as a working boat, waving its cap at the world, going by, on the way out, leaning into it at fifteen knots.

First and last, from *Hesper's* win in '86 to *Bluenose's* final defeat of Gloucester's *Gertrude L. Thebaud* in 1938, the fishermen's races have gripped the imagination, the sea call in men, the nostalgic, the sentimental. But there has never been anything on land or sea like the matches with Canada. America put her best designers and builders and mariners and schooners against their fabulous freak, the *Bluenose*, and with each victory her peppery, sawed-off little skipper Angus Walters—that brilliant sailor and tactician—waxed more quarrelsome and peevish and prideful. And Gloucester, frustrated beyond bearing it, responded in kind.

Why, such goings-on among neighbors in the Balkans would have meant a Nineteen Years' War!

These scrimmages between Gloucester and Lunenberg—between the fishing interests of New England and the Canadian Maritimes, really—have been going on longer than most people realize (and we're still at it, with the international dory races), and they haven't always been more or less friendly, either. After the Revolution John Adams in 1793 secured the rights of his countrymen to fish in Canadian waters, only to see them bargained away in 1818, after the War of 1812 with Britain, when the U.S. agreed to keep clear of Canada's three-mile limit.

For the rest of the nineteenth century these fishing rights and exclusions were rancorously contended over. Yankee hookers were chased, fired on, seized and condemned by the British and their Provincials from Cape Sable to Labrador. There was poaching, bribery and connivance, there were riots and brawls, suits, fines and jailings, investigations, commissions, indemnities and treaties.

Canadians justly resented the elbowing from Big Brother to the south, and they salted their cuts with their knowledge that Gloucester, early having run short on native talent, depended to a very large extent for the manning and the mastering of its great fleet of schooners on "whitewashed Yanks"—down-homers, as we call 'em, Nova Scotians and Newfoundlanders, bluenoses and herring chokers, master mariners attracted to the "Boston states" by a better deal fishing all around.

When *Columbia* died, seventeen of the twenty-two who died with her, including her master, were Novies.

So this was the kind of history that rode with *Bluenose*. With Angus and his bunch and all their backers and well wishers, it was just a mite more than pure sport for the hell of it, and that's a fact.

Of all the contenders for the *Halifax Herald's* gaudy cup, *Columbia* was the best we put forward. (How would *Puritan*, had she lived, and *Mayflower*, had she been allowed, made out against *Bluenose*? What would Louis and Dempsey have done to each other?) *Columbia* was built at Essex by the author's father, Arthur Dana Story, who launched *Elsie* and the *Ford* and *Shamrock* and the *Thebaud* and the *Carrie Phillips* which won the race in '87. A D. Story was Essex's most famous and prolific builder (there were 425 of them), and he was a man to be reckoned with: Dana was his ninth and last offspring, born when his Pa was sixty-five.

Dana Story spent his boyhood kicking around the shipyard, knows the whole entrancing business from keel to cap and is crazy about schooners and the sea and the old-time fishing and Essex and Gloucester and the old-time characters. In short, he is a chip off the old man, and as he did in his brilliantly evocative book about Essex shipbuilding, *Frame-Up!*, he writes with honesty and humor and a wry sort of understatement that make *Hail Columbia!* as straight and true as a shot of Bill McCoy's bootleg whiskey the boys used to land up the Essex River of a foggy early morning in the days when the heft of this yarn was spinning.

It's the real stuff, all right, and no mistake.

Now, mind yer helm, ease off jest a hair on yer fores'l, and golrammit, watch out yer don't foul that gol ram Inner Automatic sailin' through Chapter Six.

Joseph E. Garland
Eastern Point
Gloucester, Massachusetts

Foreword

The Oak Grove Cemetery in the city of Gloucester, Massachusetts, lies beside Washington Street as it goes over the rise and out towards Riverdale. Just inside the iron fence which separates the cemetery from the sidewalk, and not far from the main gate, are several family plots on which stand simple granite monuments bearing the chiselled likeness of a Gloucester schooner. On one of these appears the name "Ben Pine," and above it in the stone is a representation of the schooner *Columbia* under full press of sail and bending to a breeze of wind. Ben Pine had spoken of *Columbia* in the later years of his life as "the finest piece of wood ever to show its 'highs' out of Gloucester," and in view of his great love for fishing schooners, schooner racing and especially for his adopted city of Gloucester, it is indeed appropriate that the *Columbia* appear on his tombstone. In many ways these tombstones serve as monuments to the city of Gloucester as well as to the men lying beneath them, for these men had been the very personification of all the glorious years of Gloucester maritime history and tradition, of dory fishermen and sailing vessels and schooners racing for home. This, the racing, was the thing that particularly captured Ben Pine's imagination, and his name came to be indelibly linked with the fishermen's races, a sport of grand dimension, which for a time captured the imagination and fired the enthusiasm of a considerable segment of the whole country.

With Ben Pine's passing in 1953, all of this had come to an end. Fishing and boats were still the principal distinguishing features of Gloucester, but the character of the place was different now. It looked different, the fishing was carried on differently, the boats were different, the buildings were different—even the smells were different. The days of sailing fishermen pitting themselves and their boats against the elements in pursuit of a livelihood were over.

In the chapters of this book, we will endeavor to bring back some of that lost era; to bring back Ben Pine and his *Columbia*; to bring back the shipbuilders of Essex, Massachusetts, who created *Columbia* and so many of the others; and to bring back a brief period which was the most exciting and dramatic one the city of Gloucester ever knew.

To do this, let us take the *Columbia* and follow her life as a vessel from her conception through her building, her fishing, her racing and finally her tragic loss. Although a creature of the racing era, *Columbia*'s life was essentially the life of a typical working fisherman as carried on by generations of Gloucester men and boats. In point of fact, she proved to be the last of the sailing "salt bankers" to put out from Gloucester with no more than her sails to drive her. *Columbia* lasted four years and four months—not long, but what a life it was and what a time in which to have lived!

Before speaking of *Columbia*, we must, however, go back in time a number of years and review various events and circumstances in order to get a proper picture of the whys and wherefores of her creation. An examination of this background is most interesting, and a study of the chronology of these prior events helps in understanding how fishermen became involved with racing and how this racing assumed such prominence in the early years of the 1920s.

1 ★ Background

As part of the effort made by the city of Gloucester in 1923 to commemorate properly the three hundredth anniversary of her founding, a committee was selected to choose a suitable memorial which would best symbolize the history and tradition of the city. This committee, under the chairmanship of Carleton H. Parsons, met early in September of that year and decided that of all the ideas submitted, the design of a sculpture by Leonard Craske was most appropriate. This design depicted a Gloucester fisherman garbed in boots, sou'wester and oilskins, clutching the wheel of his schooner as he braced himself against the slanting deck. Below the figure on the stone pedestal appeared the words from the 107th Psalm: "They that go down to the sea in ships"— 1623-1923.

It would be difficult to imagine anything more appropriate. From its beginnings in 1623 Gloucester had been a community which wrested its livelihood from the sea, and its very name came to be synonymous with ships and mariners and seamanship in the most splendid of traditions. By the later decades of the nineteenth century she had become one of the greatest fishing ports of the world and her fleet of swift two-masted fishing schooners was without equal anywhere. The men who sailed in these vessels and particularly the skippers who commanded them achieved a reputation for seamanship and fortitude bordering on the charismatic. So indeed it was appropriate that "The Man at the Wheel" should be selected to symbolize the spirit of Gloucester in the years to come.

Also as part of their tercentenary celebration the people of Gloucester decided that it would be a fine thing to hold a fishermen's race. Here again the choice was wonderfully appropriate, for this could be an event which would eloquently dramatize for all to see the very substance of that spirit symbolized by their

15

statue. Moreover, in 1923, fishermen's races were uppermost in the minds of every Gloucester inhabitant. The celebration was to include the usual banquets and speakers, a parade and commemorative exercises; there was to be a fine historical pageant with scores of local participants. All this was part of the expected ritual, but the real enthusiasm and emotion of the citizens in their celebration was directed to the anniversary fishermen's race. This was something with which the average Gloucesterman could identify. It would be well at this point to see why this should be, to see why the prospect of a contest among their schooners was so exciting to the Gloucester citizenry. To do so we must review briefly the early ways of the New England fishermen and find out the origins of their apparently insatiable desire to race.

To illustrate a typical situation, let us imagine a group of schooners out on the fishing grounds. For weeks they have been jogging across the banks in their search for fish. The men in their little dories have baited and set their trawls and returned to pull in the catch. As each schooner acquired a full fare, or as they called it in Gloucester, a "trip" of fish, she hoisted sail and started for home. It was at this point that the speed and sailing ability of the vessel came to the fore. Having started, the schooner needed to gain port quickly for several reasons. First of all, certainly, was the natural urge of everyone on board to get home. Next, if the vessel had a load of fresh fish, speed was important to preserve the quality of the catch. Lastly, and most important, in the event that several vessels chanced to be sailing at about the same time, the first to arrive in port got the best price for the trip. Thus the racing by fishermen had its beginning. A brush with a sister vessel or vessels on the voyage home embraced a sizable element of sport, to be sure, but tangible rewards awaited the winner on her arrival in Gloucester, Boston, Portland or wherever. Thus we see that speed and good vessel design became at once matters of economic desirability. History has not recorded the names of the first two skippers to race to market or when they did it, but it has shown that impromptu events of this kind became something of a way of life for these men.

The natural evolution of vessel design eventually produced in

16

the New England and Nova Scotia two-masted schooner a sailing vessel with a combination of sea qualities, cargo capacity and speed unequalled anywhere at any time. In maritime and fishing circles the men who designed these ships became famous, men such as Dennison J. Lawlor, Thomas F. McManus, Bowdoin B. Crowninshield, George Melvin McClain, Edward Burgess, and his son W. Starling Burgess. Inevitably, the time came when the suggestion was put forth to hold a formal race among some boats of better reputation for the pure sport of it. The man who made the suggestion and then sponsored the race was none other than young Tom McManus, a man who at the time was in the wholesale fish business but who later was to become perhaps the best known of all the fishing vessel designers. His act earned for him in later years the appellation "Father of the Fishermen's Races."

One might suppose that Gloucester skippers and boats would have been the participants in this first race. Surprisingly, this was not the case. Each of the competing boats, and there were nine of them, was a Boston boat. Moreover, one of these, the *Hesper*, was not even a fisherman; she was a Boston pilot boat. Tom McManus was himself a Boston man and was a part owner of at least one of the contestants, the *John H. McManus*, named for his father. The others were owned by friends and fellow shipowners in the Boston fisheries.

In order to implement his idea more successfully, Mr. McManus had gone out among a number of affluent men prominent in shipping and maritime circles, and with their assistance had raised a purse of $1,500 plus the donation of a fine silver trophy by Commodore J. Malcolm Forbes, who did so with the stipulation that the Boston pilot association's *Hesper* be allowed to compete. The fishermen, however, having in mind the *Hesper's* reputation as a sailer, demurred upon hearing this, deciding they wanted no part of *Hesper*. As mediator of the dispute Mr. McManus proposed that if the pilot boat won, she could take only the trophy, the purse to go to the leading fisherman. If a fisherman won, she could take both the trophy and the purse. "You fellows are racing for money, not the cup," he told them. So they finally agreed to let *Hesper* race.

Thus on May 1, 1886, ten schooners appeared at the start of the course off Boston Light. We say ten because at the last moment the schooner *Augusta E. Herrick*, Capt. Bill Herrick of Swan's Island, Maine, showed up as an unofficial entrant and requested permission to sail over the course for the sport of sailing in a fishermen's race. She was somewhat different from the rest in that she was a center-board vessel. The official entrants were *Sarah H. Prior, John H. McManus, Gertie S. Windsor, Hattie I. Phillips, William Emerson, Belle J. Neal, Emily P. Wright, Edith Emery* and of course the *Hesper*. The skippers of these vessels were Tom McLaughlin, Johnnie O'Brien, Maurice Powers, Ned Plunket, Bat Whalen, John Driscoll, John Carney and Pat Sullivan. The skipper of *Hesper* seems not to have been recorded.

With its start off Boston Light, the triangular course went to and around Davis Ledge buoy off Minot's Light, thence to and around Half-way Rock off Marblehead and back to Boston Light. On the day of the race, the southeast wind made the first leg a dead beat to windward, the second leg a broad reach, while the third was a close reach back to the line.

After considerable maneuvering before the start, *Hesper* and *McManus* were first to cross the line, closely followed by the *Prior, Emery, Windsor* and *Phillips*. At the Davis Ledge buoy, *Hesper* was first with nearly a two-mile lead over the *McManus*, followed by *Neal, Prior, Windsor* and *Phillips*, with the rest trailing. To the next mark the wind, which had been fairly light, began to breeze up considerably and *Hesper* set her big balloon jib. The *Prior* came alive and quickly passed the *Neal* but couldn't catch the *McManus*. The *Augusta E. Herrick*, supposedly a fast vessel, picked up speed now that she was off the wind, but had dropped so far back on the beat to Minot's she could not overtake the leaders.

At Half-way Rock it was *Hesper* first, with *McManus, Prior* and *Windsor* in that order. On the last leg the breeze fell off some and all four vessels maintained their positions, finishing in the same order, giving *Hesper* the victory and the trophy and *John H. McManus* the $1,500 prize. We might say here that very likely the *Hesper*, as a pilot boat, and though about the same size as the rest, probably had a finer, more yacht-like form and a better suit of sails which her crew was more adept at handling. Speed was vital also to a pilot boat since in those days the first pilot boat on the scene was the one which got the piloting job.

Of the ten vessels, the *John H. McManus* at 111 gross tons was the biggest. The smallest ones, it turned out, made the poorest showings, which points up the time-honored axiom of sail racing that other things being equal, a good big boat will beat a good smaller boat. Another interesting point is that six of the ten contestants were the product of Essex, Massachusetts, builders.

Presumably the idea of a formally conducted race captured the enthusiasm of the fishermen, for we find that they did it again in 1887 and then in 1889. There were four boats which competed in '87, the *I. J. Merritt, Jr.*, the *John H. McManus* again, the *Carrie E. Phillips* and the *Roulette*. The *Carrie E. Phillips*, fresh from the yard of A. D. Story in Essex, was the winner. The *I. J. Merritt, Jr.*, Capt. Charlie Harty, was second, the *Roulette* third and *John H. McManus* last.

The race of 1889 was interesting in that it pitted the lovely new fisherman *Fredonia*, just built by Moses Adams at Essex, in a match race against the formidable *Hesper* for a side bet of $3,000. The *Fredonia*, sailed by Charlie Harty, was an easy victor, a result most satisfying to the fishermen.

If one reads the records of the times, one cannot help being impressed by the constant mention of racing contests among the fishermen. Most were spontaneous affairs but, as we have seen, others were more or less formally arranged, often as a result of a friendly wager. Undeniably, this competitive spirit seemed to be a part and parcel of the fisherman's life almost as much as his fishing, and reached its fullest flower in the years from perhaps 1880 to 1915, which, of course, were the years in which the sailing schooner reached its finest development.

Gloucester has always been strong on celebrations, and the celebration of 1923 was not the first one to include a fishermen's race. They had done it before in August 1892, on which occasion they celebrated the 250th anniversary of their incorporation as a town. This race of 1892 has been variously referred to over the years as "the greatest race" or "the race it blew." And so it did—over fifty miles per hour. The entrants in this race were, by common consent, some of the finest skippers and greatest sail carriers out of Gloucester. There was the *Harry L. Belden,* Capt. Maurice Whalen; the *Ethel B. Jacobs,* Capt. Sol Jacobs; the *Joseph Rowe,* Capt. Rube Cameron; the *Grayling,* Capt. Charlie Harty; the *Nannie C. Bohlin,* Capt. Tommy Bohlin; *James G. Blaine,* Capt. John McDonald; and *James S. Steele,* Capt. Charlie Olsen. The course was from a start off the whistling buoy near Eastern Point to a buoy off Half-way Rock; thence to and around Davis Ledge buoy near Minot's Light; thence back to the finish at Eastern Point, a distance of about fifty miles.

The morning of the race brought dark and chilly skies with a driving rain. The winds were approaching gale force from the northeast. It hardly seemed like August 26. The enthusiasm of the throngs of people who had come to Gloucester to witness the affair was dampened a good deal, but a great proportion of them stayed to see what they could nonetheless.

The start was scheduled for 11:00 A.M., and by ten o'clock most of the contestants were outside the harbor awaiting the start and testing the winds as they prepared themselves for whatever was in store. Despite what was now a raging northeaster, not a vessel had any reef points tied on, each skipper vowing to carry whole sail to the finish or die in the attempt. On three of the vessels, the *Jacobs,* the *Bohlin* and the *Belden,* main halyards were lashed aloft in the event that some faint-hearted crewman might suddenly be inclined to take the axe to them. One of the country's leading yachting writers, a man who had observed every type of sailing contest for over twenty-five years, said the vessels were starting "in conditions never before seen by the writer."

At the eleven o'clock whistle from the big tug used as a committee boat, it was Captain McDonald of the *James G. Blaine* who was first over the line. He was followed by the *Jacobs, Steele, Rowe, Belden, Bohlin* and *Grayling* in that order. The first leg was almost a run for the mark and the *Ethel Jacobs,* a remarkable vessel off the wind, worked out a good lead as she

20

fairly flew to the buoy off Nahant. With the weather as thick as it was, Captain Jacobs had difficulty locating the mark, going wide of the stake boat. In jibing over to round the buoy, the mainsail came over in a mighty crash which snapped the main gaff in two and rent the mainsail clear down to the boom. To all intents and purposes, this eliminated the *Ethel B. Jacobs*. Captain Sol rigged a riding sail in place of his main and completed the course, but he was out of the race.

The following vessels were quick to profit by what they had seen and used more care in rounding the mark. The *Joseph Rowe* came next, followed by the *Harry L. Belden*, the *Nannie C. Bohlin*, the *James S. Steele* and the *Grayling*. The *James G. Blaine* had already decided to give it up.

The second leg was a reach to Davis Ledge, and with decks awash, the vessels tore along for the mark. As he had from the start, Captain Whalen in his *Harry Belden* gained steadily on the others, and as they approached the Ledge was challenging Captain Cameron in the *Joseph Rowe*. All the skippers were proud and stubborn men and not one would strike any sail from his vessel though it seemed to be blowing ever harder. Someone had said before the start that the only sails to come off would be the ones the Lord took off (and He took off quite a few).

At Davis Ledge it was Rube Cameron in the *Rowe* in first place with the *Harry Belden* almost beside him. As they rounded the mark, it was both boats between buoy and ledge in a space that was supposed to leave room enough for only one. Captain Whalen had the weather berth and, quickly luffing up, was off on a port tack in the lead at last. Close behind both, however, was Tommy Bohlin in his *Nannie C.*, making heavy going but still refusing to take in sail.

From here it was to be a beat to windward all the way back to Eastern Point. The *Belden*, in the lead at last, was not to be headed. The load of fish she carried when she arrived in Gloucester the night before the race was still in her—no time to unload it—and it was just what Captain Whalen needed to hold her to it. Most of the other vessels, having had time to prepare for the race, had planned on a typical August afternoon and had taken out ballast, only to be paying dearly now for their misjudgment.

As the vessels labored across the long beat for home into the teeth of the howling northeaster, it almost seemed as if the leaders were bent on suicide rather than give in. However, the two trailing schooners had the sense to call it quits as gear was torn to shreds and the boats seemed in danger. The withdrawal of *Grayling* and the *James S. Steele* left only the *Belden, Rowe* and *Bohlin*. These schooners boiled along in a manner awesome to behold. With helmsmen lashed to the wheels they plunged again and again into seas which sent solid water clear back to the mainmasts, and rolled down repeatedly till shear poles and main hatches were in the water. Shear poles, by the way, were nearly four feet above the rail cap.

The *Belden* clung to her lead although the wind finally blew out the head sails of the *Rowe* and she fell behind, allowing Tommy Bohlin to take second spot. Try as he would he could not overtake the *Belden*. As the finish line was finally reached, the *Harry Belden*, rolling almost to her keel, was the decisive winner with the game *Nannie Bohlin* second. Limping in a poor third was Captain Cameron and the *Joseph Rowe*. An old fisherman, hanging in the weather rigging of his spectator boat to see the finish, was heard to roar as the smoke from the finish gun puffed out: "Maurice wins, he to his neck in water! The *Harry Belden* wins, the able *Harry Belden* sailin' across the line on her side an' her crew sittin' out on her keel!" Never before nor since was there a race like this and only for the fun of it too. Somebody asked Maurice Whalen a few days later if he found it rough going in the race. "It was a bit choppy," he said, "but you know the *Belden*, she likes it choppy."

Poor Captain Bohlin—it broke his heart to see his beloved *Nannie Bohlin* concede defeat. It does seem as if Tommy Bohlin deserves more than passing mention. Of all the great Gloucester skippers who have left their mark, his name always seems to be on the list of those which come most readily to mind. The characters and personalities of Tommy Bohlin and his vessel, the *Nannie C. Bohlin*, seemed naturally to complement one another. Always a great sailcarrier, he crowded his vessel unmercifully and he could usually tell to the fraction of an inch what she could stand. However, it was said that all told he carried away five sets of spars. "I drove her an' I drove her an' I drove her! Could I make her quit? The man never lived who could make the *Nannie* quit!" These were the famous words which characterized Tommy Bohlin. It was not enough that he attempted to show his heels to any vessel he encountered; he enlarged his racing to trans-Atlantic proportions.

At the time of her launching from John Bishop's Gloucester yard in October of 1890, the *Nannie C. Bohlin* at 131 gross tons was one of the port's largest vessels. She was a beautiful ship and soon established a fine reputation as a fast and able schooner while doing well in her fishing. In 1893 Captain Bohlin, himself a native Norwegian, took her clear over to Norway in search of mackerel, sailing from Newport, R. I., where he had gone for bait, to Stavanger in twenty-one days. In September he sailed for home and purposely left Norway at the same time that *Valkyrie II* left England to come over and challenge for the America's Cup. The *Nannie C. Bohlin* sailed 4,700 miles in seventeen days and on the last leg from Cape Sable to Gloucester covered the 222 nautical miles in 14 hours 25 minutes. *Valkyrie II*, sailing about 3,900 miles, made her passage in twenty-two and a half days, though in fairness it must be said that she was hove to for several days during a big gale. So it can be seen what a real Gloucester skipper could do when he put his mind to it.

About 1900 we begin to find that the yachtsmen were taking a serious interest in the abilities of sailing fishermen. It's no wonder, for the fishermen, long scornful of the fancy boats, clothes and ways of yachtsmen, had for years seized every opportunity for a brush with the big schooner yachts. More often than not it was the fisherman who was the easy victor. In coming across Massachusetts Bay with a trip of fish many years back, Capt. Tom McLaughlin in the *Sarah H. Prior* had overtaken and literally sailed in rings twice around a big schooner yacht, after which he continued on to Boston. The yachtsman was so disgusted with his boat that as soon as he reached Boston he went straight up to his yacht broker and ordered his vessel to be sold.

Rather curiously, it might seem, the city of Boston held an "Old Home Celebration" in 1901. Perhaps borrowing a leaf from Gloucester's book, they held a "grand fishermen's race" for which the noted Thomas W. Lawson (of seven-master fame) generously provided the trophies. There were two classes, A and B, for larger and smaller boats. Winner of class A was the *Benjamin F. Phillips*, Capt. Maurice Powers; second was *Priscilla Smith*, Capt. William Corkum; third and last *Navahoe*, Capt. Marty Welch. In the smaller class only two vessels sailed; *Manomet* was first and *Mattakeesett* second.

The last of the fine contests held before the era of international competition took place off Boston in the summer of 1907, for a trophy donated by none other than the great Sir Thomas Lipton, whose five *Shamrocks* challenged unsuccessfully for the America's Cup. (Another competition for the Lipton Cup was to come in 1923, but more of that later.) Three big schooners took part: the *Rose Dorothea* and *Jessie Costa* of Provincetown and the *James W. Parker* of Boston. An easy victor was the *Rose Dorothea* who, in spite of a broken fore topmast which carried away her fore gaff topsail and flying jib, maintained her lead over the *Jessie Costa*. The element of size was again a factor in the victory of the *Rose Dorothea*. She was a vessel of 145 gross tons and 109 foot waterline as against 130 gross tons and approximately 102 foot waterline for each of the others.

So far as racing is concerned, we here come to the end of what some like to think of as the "age of innocence." In the light of events which were to come in the realm of fishermen's races, these had been satisfying and one might say happy times. The vessels which raced did so in something of a spirit of exuberance and *joie de vivre* and for the sport of the competition. Any particular preparation for the more formal contests was slight. Vessels usually discharged their fish and tidied up a bit and that was all. Sometimes they didn't even bother to do that. It was a boat-for-boat, "come as you are" proposition with their regular working crews sailing to the only rules they ever sailed by. To the fishermen, the only important racing was the racing for market, and if a vessel was able to get out to the banks fast, get in a good trip of fish and get home safely and fast, she was a good vessel.

2 ★ 1920-1921

In the fall of 1920, William H. Dennis, as publisher and spokesman of his newspapers, the *Halifax* (Nova Scotia) *Herald* and
Evening Mail, offered to provide a trophy to be awarded the
winner of a race or series of races between the best of the Nova
Scotia fishing fleet and the best from Massachusetts. No doubt
he had in mind that such an event could accomplish many things:
it would create a sporting spectacle to stir the imagination; it
would stimulate an awareness of and interest in the fisheries of
both Canada and the United States; it might possibly bolster
Canadian national pride if they beat the Yankees at something;
and perhaps it just might be good for the newspaper business.
Somebody in the background also said something about promot-
ing improvements in fishing vessel design.

In both countries the fishing industries were carried on in much
the same way in boats which were basically similar. Furthermore
the city of Lunenburg, N.S., was closely parallel in nature and
characteristics to Gloucester, Massachusetts. Each ultimately was
to go all out for the honor of the homeland and the local fleet.
No one could deny that the idea of such a contest between these
honest toilers of the sea from two great countries sailing in such
magnificent and world-renowned craft was one of truly noble
proportion, the *sine qua non* of ocean racing. True, the yachtsmen from England and New York had been doing something
like this for the last sixty-nine years, but they were yachtsmen.
This was to be the real thing, a contest between some of the
world's finest professional mariners sailing in real working vessels, not just racing machines designed to be sailed once and
then broken up for scrap. Who could mention a yachting contest
in the same breath with something like this? Remember how
Tommy Bohlin outsailed *Valkyrie II* in their race across the

26

Atlantic. When you're talking about Gloucester or Lunenburg, you're talking about something in a class by itself.

In the issue of the *Gloucester Daily Times* for Friday, October 1, 1920, there appeared on an inside page a small item to the effect that citizens and businessmen of Halifax, N.S., had subscribed to date a total of $2,240 for prizes to be awarded the winner of a fisherman's race from Lunenburg to Halifax. The race was to be held as an event of the Halifax Commercial and Sports Carnival. The article went on to state that the race was looked on by some observers as a preliminary to an international contest proposed several weeks ago between a Nova Scotia boat and a representative of the New England fleet. It would appear, perhaps, that Gloucester did not hear the alarm go off since no further mention of the event appears for nearly two weeks, but on Wednesday, October 13, the *Times* carried the story of a challenge to an international race, the winner to be declared champion of the North Atlantic. It stated that a committee had been gathered in Halifax to map the details of such an event and that it was proposed to sail the race over a forty-mile course off Halifax for a $5,000 purse, $4,000 for the winner and $1,000 for the loser. The conditions would be as follows:

1. Vessel must be a bona fide fisherman with at least one year's experience on the banks.

2. Vessels must carry inside ballast only.

3. Sails used in the race to be made of ordinary commercial duck and to be of no greater area than those in ordinary use on the banks and to be limited to mainsail, foresail, jumbo, jib, jib topsail, fore and main working gaff topsails and fisherman's staysail.

4. Crew to be limited to twenty-five men.

5. Skipper to be a bona fide fishing captain with at least one year's experience on the banks.

6. Vessels to be not more than 150 feet over-all length.

7. Race to be sailed boat for boat without any time allowance.

8. Decisions of sailing committee, on which both sides are to be represented, to be regarded as final in the interpretation of above conditions.

9. Trophy to be awarded to the winner of the best two out of three races.

On that same day (Wednesday, October 13) which saw the issuance of the challenge, the Canadians themselves were holding an elimination race to pick their own representative. Nine boats sailed a neck and neck contest which was won by the *Delawana* of Lunenburg. (The Lunenburg fleet alone numbered 120 vessels.)

Now Gloucester suddenly became wide awake and leaped to the challenge in something of a "why didn't we think of this before" attitude. As it had been requested that a reply be received in seven days, Gloucester was thrown into a bit of a turmoil. The trend towards elimination of sail through the installation of auxiliary engines was well under way in the Gloucester fleet by 1920, and the number of sailing schooners suitable for racing was dwindling fast. Moreover, many of the vessels which might have been considered as entrants were out fishing when the challenge was received. The problem, then, for Gloucester was to decide as best it could what vessel could (and would) enter. Several vessels were proposed but none seemed exactly suitable. Ben Smith of the Gorton-Pew Company came forward now and offered one of his vessels, the *Esperanto*, just in from a trip. It seemed a happy solution as the *Esperanto* had the reputation of being a good sailer and easily met the qualifications; she was immediately available and could be gotten ready with a minimum of time and effort.

So, having a challenger, Gloucester, on Saturday, October 16, wired her acceptance and the race was on. It did seem a shame that there was not more time to prepare. The Canadians had had an elimination race to pick their boat which now would be all tuned up when the *Esperanto* arrived. But if enthusiasm would win for Gloucester, the *Delawana* was already beaten. The city was galvanized into action with everyone who could contributing something to the preparations.

The *Esperanto* was a fairly old boat, having come from the Essex yards of James and Tarr back in June, 1906. As she was just arrived from the banks she needed a little scrubbing up, so with the discharge of fish and fishing gear she was hauled out on the railways while the gang turned to with a vengeance to make her ready. The propeller came off and the propeller shaft was taken out, the hull was smoothed and painted and all minor repairs attended to. Back in the water, her old skipper, Charlie Harty, the man who had taken her fishing when she was new, supervised the placing of eighty-five tons of ballast to give her a good sailing trim. She had been designed as a seiner by Washington Tarr of the James and Tarr firm, using the proven characteristics of McManus origin. She was known as a good sailer, especially by the wind, but it was felt that with such a short time to prepare, the Americans would be sailing at a considerable disadvantage. The *Delawana*, on the other hand, was subject to enough spit and polish for a yacht and her tune-up racing and practice had brought her to a peak of racing trim. But there was no time in Gloucester to worry about that.

On Monday a delegation including Mr. Dennis of the Halifax papers, donor of the cup, arrived in town to talk things over with the ad hoc committee which had hastily been gathered to superintend the city's efforts. It developed that a couple of new rules had crept into the list. They prohibited the shifting of any ballast after the preparatory gun and limited the time for the race to nine hours. Furthermore, it was disclosed that course and racing conditions would be decided by a committee of the Royal Nova Scotia Yacht Squadron on which the Americans would have representation. However, the Halifax committee wanted it known that hard and fast rules of yachting would be tabooed and that it would be a practical race between fishermen in which regular rules of the road as fishermen knew them would prevail. It was the desire of all in charge that crews as well as skippers be real fishermen and that employment of yachtsmen and other outside experts would be frowned upon.

Meanwhile, down at the wharf, the *Esperanto* was being prepared as best it could be. (After all, a vessel that had been fishing for fourteen years was no bed of roses.) The committee decided that Capt. Martin Welch would be the skipper with Capt. John Matheson as mate and Isaiah Gosbee as cook.The rest of the crew of twenty-five included five other captains as well as author James B. Connolly. It was reported that *Delawana's* crew would consist only of captains, led by her regular skipper Capt. Tommy Himmelman. The handsome trophy donated by the *Halifax Herald* was all ready and waiting to be awarded to the winner, and excitement in Gloucester (and all New England) as well as in Nova Scotia was rapidly reaching a fever pitch. In Digby, N.S., the natives couldn't make up their minds for whom to root. Naturally they wanted the Canadian boat to win but still, Marty Welch, the Yankee skipper, was a Digby boy—born and raised there—and it posed a difficult decision.

At last all was ready and on Monday, October 25, *Esperanto* sailed for Halifax amid a wild send-off. Every vantage point about the harbor was crowded with the Gloucester faithful to wave on their champion. The run to Nova Scotia was mostly against head winds and took fifty-one hours. In Halifax it was announced that the *Herald's* cup would become a perpetual challenge trophy open to yearly competition.

The first race started at 9 A.M. on Saturday, October 30, over the forty-mile triangular course off Halifax. There was a fairly good breeze. *Delawana* was first over the line and was leading at the first mark, but with freshening winds Marty was steadily closing the gap and, before the second mark, had taken a good lead. It was *Esperanto's* race all the way from then on, showing a definite superiority over *Delawana* in all points of sailing. At the finish it was *Esperanto* by 18 minutes and 28 seconds.

The next day was Sunday—no race. *Delawana's* crew spent the day in a desperate attempt to remove and shift ballast. It was hoped that by taking out a sizable amount the vessel would be faster in light airs, gambling, of course, that they would get their light airs. Marty was perfectly satisfied with *Esperanto* and enjoyed his day of rest.

At race time the next day, November 1, it appeared that *Delawana's* gamble had paid off. The winds were much lighter than they had been on Saturday, and with reduced ballast and a hull two feet shallower than *Esperanto,* she took the lead right after the start and held it—at least for thirty miles she held it. Occasionally *Esperanto* would threaten, only to fall back again. In the light airs it seemed that today it was to be *Delawana's* turn. However, Marty hung on and doggedly pressed every ounce of his skill to the pursuit of *Delawana.*

Suddenly, about two o'clock, the winds increased with squalls of rain, and the picture changed. Marty was able to bring his vessel up to within striking distance. In a nip and tuck situation first one vessel then the other held a momentary advantage. A luffing match developed with *Delawana* attempting to gain the weather berth. They had passed the third mark now, and in the struggle to maintain the advantage, *Delawana* was crowding *Esperanto* close to Devil's Island. Both vessels were heading dangerously near the shoal water over the ledges. Still Marty would not be shaken off. The Canadian pilot put aboard to guide *Esperanto* was beginning to look a little pale as on they headed. Worse, she was drawing some two feet more than *Delawana.*

"Skipper," he called, "we're standing in too close!"

"Skipper!" came the voice of Micky Hall from the crosstrees. "I can see the rocks and kelp!"

On deck, crewman Russell Smith, representing his father and the owners of *Esperanto*, sang out, "To hell with the rocks and kelp, Marty. Keep 'er to it!"

At this the pilot hailed Captain Himmelman for sea room, and good skipper that he was, Captain Himmelman bore off to make way for *Esperanto*. It cost him a length or so to get out of the way, and at once *Esperanto* squeezed past *Delawana* and the rocks and into good water again. As they rounded the last buoy, *Delawana's* bowsprit was almost over the *Esperanto's* taffrail.

From here to the finish the wind breezed up still more and storm clouds rolled in. It was a dead beat for the last seven miles to the line and just what *Esperanto* wanted. She gained steadily and at the gun was the winner by 7 minutes and 25 seconds.

Back in Gloucester, all who could were crowded into the little Western Union office to keep in touch with the news from Halifax. Among them was Ben Smith of the Gorton-Pew firm who, perhaps more than anyone, had made it possible for Gloucester to challenge by offering *Esperanto* for competition. When news of the victory came over the telegraph, the operator handed it first to him, and reaching for the telephone he called the cold storage plant to give them a simple message: "Blow your whistle!" That's all it took. Gloucester fell apart in a delirium of joy.

The *Esperanto* came home with a new broom at her masthead and the beautiful big silver cup stowed in the main hold. Marty and the crew were the heroes of the hour. On Monday, November 9, two weeks after they had sailed for Halifax, Gloucester held a monster banquet in the state armory to honor her men; even Governor Calvin Coolidge was there. "A triumph for Americanism," he said.

It was a good victory for Gloucester, for the *Esperanto* and for Marty Welch. The races had been well and skillfully sailed with good sportsmanship displayed on both sides. Captain Himmelman and his men took their defeat in good grace. There was no question here that both vessels held to the spirit as well as the letter of the rules. As remarkably close in size as they were, it was shown that *Esperanto* was a better boat for a strong breeze, while *Delawana* was better in light airs and her crew seemed to be able to handle sail more quickly. Unlike Captain Himmelman who was commanding his own ship, Marty Welch had never before sailed on the *Esperanto* until taking her to Halifax. But he brought the Dennis Cup to Gloucester, and they took it up and put it in a window on Main Street for everybody to see.

Following the races the donor of the trophy met with his associates in Halifax to draft a proper Deed of Gift. The terms and regulations agreed to were immediately published in Gloucester. They made interesting reading. Following are some of the more salient points.

It was provided, first of all, that the trophy was to be administered by a group of nine Trustees, all of whom were to be Canadians. One was to be the premier of Nova Scotia and one was to be the mayor of Halifax, with seven other men. Any vacancies were to be filled by a majority of the remaining Trustees.

The races were to be under the control and management of an

32

International Race Committee of five to be elected for each series of races. The Trustees were to pick two, the governor of Massachusetts in conjunction with the local committee would pick two, and the chairman was to be picked by the two members representing the country where the races were to be held.

Vessels must be bona fide fishing vessels who have been fishing for at least *one season* previous to the race.

All vessels to be propelled by sails only and not to exceed 125 feet in length over-all. No outside ballast to be used and draft not to exceed sixteen feet.

Vessels shall race with the same spars and with no greater sail area than used in fishing, but sail area not to exceed 80% of the square of the water line length as expressed in square feet.

No ballast shall be shifted after the fifteen-minute preparatory gun.

Course shall not be less than thirty-five nor more than forty nautical miles with a time limit for each race of nine hours. There shall be no handicap or time allowance.

Sailing committee to be a sub-committee of the international committee and shall be an independent body having no financial interest in either vessel.

Lastly, the Deed of Gift said: "The trustees of the trophy shall have the power to modify any detail of the rules, but shall do nothing that will change the spirit of the intention of the donors —that the races shall be confined to vessels and crews engaged in practical commercial fishing."

The loss by the *Delawana* of this first series in international competition stung the Canadians. The Yankees in an old vessel just in from the banks had come up and beaten them at their own game and in their own front yard. This would never do; the trophy must be brought home. To do so, a syndicate of concerned men in Lunenburg and Halifax organized themselves and proceeded at once to lay their plans. An able young Halifax naval architect, William J. Roué, was engaged and instructed to address himself to the problem. This he did, and on December 19, 1920, the Duke of Devonshire, Governor-General of Canada, was assisted in driving the first bolt in the keel of a splendid new schooner in the Smith and Rhuland shipyard at Lunenburg, Nova Scotia. She was to be a big one, too, bigger than the average schooner of Lunenburg registry, though not what could be described as exceptional. (There were twenty-two schooners of Lunenburg registry in 1921 bigger than this one.) It would appear that the hull dimensions outlined in the Deed of Gift must have been changed to fit the new schooner, for her over-all length was to be 143 feet, instead of 125 as previously stated, with a waterline length of 112. The Deed of Gift now listed an over-length not to exceed 150 feet with a waterline length of 112. (When originally proposed, a length of 150 feet was specified.)

Construction of the vessel was watched with interest and enthusiasm through the winter of 1921, and when launching day came on March 26, over 6,000 people gathered in the yard to cheer as Miss Audrey Smith, daughter of one of the yard owners, Richard Smith, christened the *Bluenose*. Miss Smith was also a niece of Angus Walters, the man who was to be skipper of the new vessel. Photographs of the event show at least twenty two-masted sailing schooners lying at anchor in Lunenburg harbor.

All this had not escaped the attention of people on the American side of the border. A number of men prominent in business and maritime circles in and about Boston were of the opinion that "if they can do it, we can do it too" and to this end formed their own syndicate, calling themselves the Mayflower Associates. The terms of the Deed of Gift had not been made public in this country until early November, and for the group to design and build a vessel and have her on her way to the fishing banks by April 30, as the deed specified, was not going to be easy.

The Associates sought the services of one of America's foremost yacht designers, W. Starling Burgess, who drew up plans for a schooner to be called *Mayflower*. These were taken to the J. F. James and Son yard in Essex, Massachusetts, and construction was started at once. To meet the deadline, every man in the yard plus an extra gang of men from East Boston was pressed into service, and the *Mayflower* was completed in fifty-nine working days.

She, too, was a big vessel, actually somewhat bigger than *Bluenose*. She measured 164 gross tons to *Bluenose's* 153 and showed a registered length of 131.6 feet to *Bluenose's* 130.2. Both boats drew about sixteen feet of water although *Bluenose* showed a little more beam, 27.0 to *Mayflower's* 25.8. In sail area they were about the same. The Canadians were watching all this, and for some time prior to *Mayflower's* launching, murmurings were heard in the direction of Halifax. It was wondered out loud whether she was going to be a genuine fisherman or was she, perhaps, just a fisherman-style yacht. Rumor had it that she would never be allowed to compete.

The *Mayflower's* owners, well aware of this talk, attempted to clarify matters by inviting the Trustees to send a delegation to look over the vessel for themselves and also to attend the launching while they were here. The Canadians arrived via the Yarmouth boat on April 11 and were surprised to be met at the wharf by Wilmot Reed, secretary of the Gloucester committee. At this point the *Mayflower* men showed up and we read that something of a rhubarb developed between the Boston and Gloucester camps. It ended with the Boston hosts snatching the Nova Scotia delegates away in a taxicab for the Parker House while Mr. Reed stood in chagrin upon the wharf.

The next day was launching day at Essex. The old shipbuilding town had never seen anything like it. The police estimated that there were over 8,000 people in attendance. Present were Mayor Peters of Boston, Charles Francis Adams, George Lawley, the famous yacht builder, and from Canada, H. G. Lawrence, F. W. Baldwin and *Bluenose* designer William J. Roué. These last were the men who could decide *Mayflower's* eligibility to compete for the Dennis Cup. The bottle of champagne was wielded by little Miss Starling Burgess, daughter of the designer. The launching went well but the formalities had taken so long that the tide in the little Essex River had begun to drop, and as *Mayflower* was taken in tow by the tug *Sadie Ross* for the trip to Boston, she became ignominiously stuck on a mudbank about a half mile from the yard and had to stay there until the next day. Perhaps it was an omen of things to come.

Parenthetically, we might note that the building of *Bluenose* and *Mayflower* was also being watched by many interested although perhaps more objective observers. We find in the record an increasing frequency of comment deploring the obvious attempts to divorce the international fishermen's races from the purpose for which they were originally designed. An editorial making this very point had appeared in a New York paper in late March. The *Halifax Herald*, somewhat self-consciously it seemed, itself took notice of these comments and went on to say that the competing schooners must be fishermen whether built in Lunenburg or Boston. It said they couldn't go out to the grounds and just "lounge around" complying with the letter but not the spirit of the Deed of Gift. It said further that new vessels of an apparently radical design must not be frowned upon and concluded by saying: "Let the competing schooners be any type conforming to the regulations of the contest, but they must first, last and always be fishermen."

The "radical design" bit was an obvious reference to the somewhat radical design Mr. Burgess had given to the stern of *Mayflower*. Nothing like it had hitherto been seen on a fisherman, and it did, unfortunately, give the vessel a yachty appearance. Other yacht-like features were a dolphin-striker and broad upswept laminated spreaders. These were, therefore, the subject of considerable comment and speculation. In any case the gentlemen from Canada looked her over very carefully and went home to report that in their opinion there was no substantial difference between the construction of this boat and that of other American fishermen. The Trustees therefore said that whether *Mayflower* raced or not would be up to the American selection committee.

Mayflower was towed to Boston, where she was rigged and outfitted with all haste and in two weeks was ready for a trial run. The guest list for this occasion read like a page from Who's Who in American yachting. During her brief stay at the Boston wharf she had been a mecca for thousands of sightseers and people anxious to have a look at the splendid vessel which, it was hoped, would be the new defender of the Dennis Cup.

On April 28, in command of her skipper J. Henry Larkin, she

cleared Boston on her maiden voyage, going first to Gloucester, from which she sailed for Shelburne, N. S. Several vessels had been looking for a brush with the elegant new speedster and a challenge for a race to Shelburne was issued by Capt. Felix Hogan in the new schooner *L. A. Dunton.* But "pride goeth before a fall," they say, and *L. A. Dunton* was beaten by seven hours on the trip. *Mayflower,* it was reported, handled beautifully. Captain Hogan wouldn't concede and challenged again for the next leg of the voyage to Canso. Again he was soundly beaten. This time he gave up. On the last legs of her maiden voyage, *Mayflower* went to Souris, P. E. I., and from there to the Magdalen Islands, from which she departed for the banks.

While all this was taking place, *Bluenose* also had sailed on her own maiden trip to La Have and, like *Mayflower,* found sister vessels lying in wait for an informal contest. It was acutely embarrassing for her to be beaten on the trip by no less than four schooners of uncertain age and condition, a circumstance that occasioned a measure of distress to the 100 or more people holding shares in her.

Bluenose was not the only Canadian effort made that year in quest of the fishermen's trophy. Mayor Amos Pentz of Shelburne was trying it too. Mayor Pentz, a man of seventy-one, was a shipbuilder by profession, and he built a big schooner of his own named *Canadia* in the hope of becoming the challenger. *Canadia* competed in the elimination races that fall, coming in second to *Bluenose* in the first race. However, she was declared ineligible to challenge officially for the trophy since her waterline length was close to 116 feet, four feet too many. The result was a very indignant town of Shelburne.

In mid-May came ominous rumblings from the *Halifax Herald* as to whether *Mayflower* had really complied with the Deed of Gift. It seemed that someone had uncovered a rumor that *Mayflower* was to be sold as a yacht after the fall races; moreover, it understood that certain items of equipment, notably a proper anchor cable, were not on board, and, most distressing of all, it noted that *Mayflower* was taking an awfully long time getting to the banks. Other Nova Scotians rather unkindly intimated that

37

in their view *Mayflower* was not a real fisherman at all but only a "toy boat." *Mayflower's* owners were quick to respond by offering to compete with *Bluenose* in a winter race the following January. They also bluntly stated that in their opinion much of the complaint against *Mayflower* was originating in Gloucester, not Halifax. They contended that Gloucester was jealous and had no desire to see a Boston boat in defense of the trophy, to which Gloucester was quick to reply in effect: "Not so. We merely pointed out that the Deed of Gift clearly states that 'a vessel must have left her last port of call for the banks by April 30.' *Mayflower* never left Boston until April 28 and then went all those places after that." As if to calm the troubled waters, came the voice of designer Roué from Halifax saying that *Bluenose* was not afraid of *Mayflower*. Though the center of a storm of controversy, *Mayflower* carried on her season's fishing and acquired at the same time an impressive reputation for speed, since she took all comers and beat them.

As a preliminary to the big contests, it had been planned to hold an elimination race in the fall to select the official defender, and *Mayflower*, having made application, was duly accepted by the Gloucester committee. However, it developed that if *Mayflower* was to be in it, no Gloucester boat would apply, so the committee, therefore, nominated *Mayflower* to be the American defender. At this the Trustees in Halifax dropped their bomb. On September 15 they ruled *Mayflower* to be in violation of the spirit as well as the letter of the Deed of Gift, saying that they believed her to be in reality a schooner-yacht. So—no *Mayflower*. The Gloucester committee was quick to follow suit and the very next day declared that in view of the action of the trustees, *Mayflower* was thereby disqualified.

It might be said at this point that few events in the sporting history of this country have generated a higher degree of acrimonious and impassioned debate than the business of *Bluenose* vs. *Mayflower* and the subsequent ruling by the Trustees. Even all this turned out to be but the opening episodes in a drama that was to continue for seventeen more years. The issues raised by it will even now stir a discussion in Gloucester or Lunenburg and will probably never be settled satisfactorily.

With *Mayflower* out of the way, it now became necessary to hold an American elimination race. This took place on October 12 with five entrants: *Ralph Brown, Elsie G. Silva, Arthur James, Philip P. Manta* and *Elsie*. (Gloucester's great old *Esperanto* was no longer around, having gone to her doom on Sable Island the previous May.) Certainly none among these boats could be described as anything but a bona fide fisherman. Not one of them was less than five years old, and the *Philip P. Manta* from Provinceton had been built in 1902. Although *Esperanto* was gone, Marty Welch was still very much alive and as skipper of the *Elsie* was an easy winner.

Like *Esperanto, Elsie* was a real and typical fishing schooner. She had come from the Essex yard of Arthur D. Story in May of 1910. Designed by Tom McManus, she was a medium sized vessel with an over-all length of 120 feet, a beam of thirteen feet four inches and a gross tonnage of 135. It is interesting to note that she had begun her career as a Boston boat and in 1919 had been transferred to the Canadian division of the Gorton-Pew firm, being registered under the British flag in Lunenburg. She had come back to Gloucester that very summer.

In Canada they ran an elimination series for the best two out of three. There were eight contestants. *Bluenose* won the first race by a good four minutes over *Canadia* and in the second it was *Bluenose* by fifteen minutes over *Delawana*. Angus Walters had taken his first victory; now it was *Elsie's* turn.

A careful comparison of the statistics on the two vessels would have shown, even before she left, that as far as racing was concerned, *Elsie* was only going to Halifax for the ride. She was hopelessly outclassed by *Bluenose,* which was a full twenty-three feet longer, two and a half feet wider, drew better than a foot and a half more water and spread a good 1,500 square feet more canvas. That she performed as well as she did was a tribute to the skill of Marty Welch, who strove mightily to get all he could from his smaller vessel. But the best of Marty and the *Elsie* were no match for a giant like the *Bluenose.*

Halifax welcomed the *Elsie* on Thursday, October 20, after a forty-eight-hour passage from Gloucester. It didn't take long after their arrival for the caliber of the opposition to sink home to Marty and the crew. They found that it was practically impossible to have a close look at the rival *Bluenose* since she was tied up in the naval dockyard across the harbor. She and her crew had been busy with drills in sail-handling and tacking ship under the direction of a lieutenant commander of the Royal Canadian Navy. He had heard that Marty and his men were fast sail-handlers and he wanted to instill some Navy discipline into his men. It further turned out that the rules now allowed thirty men in the crew, so *Elsie*'s complement of twenty-six men was increased with the addition of Capt. John Morash and Ben Pine.

On Friday it was scheduled that the contestants would be hauled out for official measurements and inspection, and *Elsie* was duly put on the railway and measured to the satisfaction of all concerned. Many people took advantage of the opportunity to look her over. With *Bluenose* it seemed to be a little different. With blocking set for a draft of sixteen feet, they couldn't seem to get her on the carriage, so after several tries the effort was abandoned. The dockmaster said she must have been drawing close to seventeen feet, though the Deed of Gift said a vessel must not exceed sixteen. This was cause for some worry among the Gloucester people, since they had also picked up a few rumors that *Bluenose* was a little strong on waterline length.

Anyway, Saturday was the day of the first race and at nine o'clock they were off. *Bluenose* had left her dock at 7:00 A.M. to give the crew time for a little more drill. With plenty of wind, which at times was reaching thirty knots, *Elsie* was first over the line and proceeded to give an excellent account of herself. She led a good part of the way, showing herself to be faster on a run. Considering her size, she was doing amazingly well when midway through the course her fore topmast carried away, taking the fore gaff topsail and balloon jib with it. With *Elsie* plunging into the seas as she was, Harry Christansen, the big Norwegian rigger from Gloucester, and six of his mates went out on the diving bowsprit to bring in the ballooner and clear the wreckage.

Under reduced sail and by the wind now, *Elsie* fell back. In fairness Angus dowsed his topsails too, but the superiority of *Bluenose*, even under reduced rig, was clearly evident. *Bluenose* won by 9 minutes 31 seconds.

Repairs were made over Sunday and *Bluenose* was finally hauled for measurements at the request of the Americans. On Monday they tried again. Once more *Elsie* got off to a good start and led *Bluenose* for nearly two-thirds of the distance, but again she was beaten on the windward legs of the course. *Bluenose's* margin of victory was almost exactly what it had been in the first race, 9 minutes 30 seconds. An unexpected sidelight of this race was the appearance of none other than *Mayflower*, which fell in with the contestants for a considerable distance. With her winter rig of just the four big lowers and with a full load of dories and fishing gear, she easily held her own.

However, rather than interfere with the progress of the contestants, *Mayflower* turned aside and dropped back after the second turn. The men of *Elsie* and *Mayflower* were impressed, in looking over the *Bluenose* after the series, by the spit and polished appearance she presented. Here was a vessel supposed to be a fisherman decked out in shiny brass trim and sail covers and having electric lights and electric signal bells. Her rigging in every way was lighter than *Mayflower's*, with even the ratlines removed to cut down windage.

Thus with her first victory in the international competition *Bluenose* and Angus Walters had brought the trophy back to Canada. It was time for the post-mortems. Agreement was universal that *Elsie* and her men had given an excellent account of themselves. During her periods of lying at the wharf in Halifax, *Elsie* had been visited by thousands of Canadians, many of whom were most outspoken in their admiration. Quite surprising, too, were the many who frankly stated that in their opinion it had been a fear of *Mayflower* which prompted the action of the Trustees as well as the fact that many of *Mayflower's* shares were held by yachtsmen and others having no connection with the fishing industry.

41

In the United States it was felt that basic questions of fairness were involved; in short, what was sauce for the goose should have been sauce for the gander, and if *Mayflower* was to be labeled a yacht, *Bluenose* most certainly should have been, too. It was hard for most Americans to see where there was any particular difference between the two; moreover, it somehow seemed that everything was working to the advantage of the Canadians. In Gloucester, as far as this case was concerned, sentiment seemed to be that it was better to have had *Elsie* go to Halifax and lose than enter *Mayflower* and have her win after all the disputations and recriminations of the past season.

Quite admittedly *Mayflower* had been built to be a successful challenger for the Dennis Trophy, but so also had been the *Bluenose*. Quite admittedly the *Mayflower* was possessed of some design features which were not commonly seen on fishermen, but the *Halifax Herald* itself had said that new vessels of radical design must not be frowned on and *Mayflower* had proved her ability as a fisherman by working all summer. Moreover, if anyone was a bona fide fisherman, Capt. Henry Larkin was. From the American side of the border, it looked as though the Trustees were changing the rules during the game to produce a "heads I win, tails you lose" type of contest. Yet in spite of this was the unsettling recollection among some Americans that Gloucester itself had been more than a little instrumental in the rejection of the *Mayflower*. It had covertly planted suspicion as to *Mayflower*'s eligibility and more significantly had made no real effort to defend its selection of *Mayflower* as the American entrant following her rejection by the Canadians. Her owners could hardly be blamed for their bitterness, having long expressed their desire to at least give the public a real contest. The immediate acceptance by the Gloucester committee of the Canadian decision had spoken louder than words.

3 * The Series of 1922

As the Canadians had been stung by their defeat at the hands of Marty Welch in the *Esperanto,* so now was Gloucester's pride wounded with the trimming administered to their *Elsie* by Angus Walters and his *Bluenose.* With the completion of the first race on Saturday it was painfully apparent to the Gloucester delegation that, as expected, the *Elsie* was a sure loser. It was also remembered that as matters now stood there was no other vessel in Gloucester even remotely able to stand up to *Bluenose.* With fierce determination to do what they could to bring the trophy back to Gloucester, a group of men gathered for dinner that evening in a Halifax hotel. Seated about the table were Capt. Jeff Thomas and his brother Bill, Kenneth Ferguson of the Gloucester National Bank, Marion Cooney of United Sail Loft, Mr. Fulham of the Fulham Fish Co., and Ben Pine. Ben had skippered the *Philip P. Manta* in the elimination race and was presently a crew member of *Elsie*; at home he headed the newly established Atlantic Supply Co., a firm of vessel operators and ship chandlers. As they discussed the situation, they resolved to band themselves together in a syndicate to build a proper challenger for the following year.

Upon returning to Gloucester the group was joined by Philip P. Manta of Boston, owner of the schooner of the same name, and eight others, including several skippers. They elected to call their organization the Manta Club. Reasoning that he was the best man available, they too commissioned W. Starling Burgess to design their vessel. He produced a set of lines strongly resembling those of *Mayflower,* though a little smaller and with perhaps just a little more fullness through the body. This time he gave the schooner a traditional fisherman's transom stern. The result was the *Puritan,* named for the America's Cup defender of 1885. She was built that winter in the James yard at Essex. Ready in good season, she was launched on March 15, 1922, after christening by Miss Ray Adams, a business associate of Ben Pine. Her skipper was to be Capt. Jeff Thomas, one of the partners and owner of the largest share. He was noted as a great carrier and had been a protégé of the famous Marty Welch. As the spars were being stepped, Captain Thomas placed a five-dollar gold piece beneath each mast for good luck.

Puritan was a handsome big schooner carrying eleven dories and a crew of twenty-five. She had a rather short bowsprit and a fairly lofty rig. Her sails, measuring about 9,000 square feet in area, were made by Marion Cooney's United Sail Loft. In use she was found to be very fast and rather tricky to handle. On several occasions she reeled off speeds of better than fifteen knots.

She left Gloucester on her maiden trip on April 17 to the blasts of factory whistles and the horns of scores of sister craft in the harbor. From Lufkin and Tarr's wharf came a salute of three cannon shots. As she left the harbor an accompanying dragger logging eleven knots was forced to fall far behind, unable to keep up to the flying *Puritan*. The first night out was spent in Provincetown. She left the next morning for Edgartown, where she planned to take on bait. Off Cape Cod, Jeff Thomas met his old friend Captain Larkin of the *Mayflower*, who had been lying in wait for just such an encounter. Naturally, a race was on, and for the only time in her life, *Mayflower* was left in the distance.

The *Puritan* made two trips halibuting that spring and was outward bound on her third when, on the night of June 23, at a speed of twelve knots and under full sail, she piled onto the northwest bar of Sable Island, a total loss. Captain Thomas and all but one of the crew were saved. The hopes and aspirations of the Manta Club were thus cruelly dashed and a vessel which had borne such great promise as a contender had met a sudden and most untimely end after a life of little more than three months. There must have been something wrong with Captain Thomas's gold pieces.

As far as having a new contender was concerned, all was not lost for Gloucester. While Everett James was building *Puritan* in his yard, another possible contender was taking shape across the Essex River in Arthur D. Story's yard. This was Capt. Clayton Morrissey's new schooner the *Henry Ford*. Captain Clayt, a rather quiet and businesslike man, was admired in Gloucester as an able skipper and a good fisherman. The time had come for a new vessel and he had decided it might just as well be a schooner suitable for competition, so he had Tom McManus design the *Henry Ford*. (Just why he picked the name *Henry Ford* seems not to have been recorded.)

In general dimensions the *Puritan* and the *Henry Ford* were very close, each having an over-all length of about 139 feet. *Puritan* had a greater registered length, but *Ford* was three feet longer on the waterline and had a few inches more beam. She also had a slightly taller rig and carried about 500 square feet more sail. *Puritan* measured out to 149 gross tons and *Ford* 155. Both vessels were smaller than *Mayflower*.

Tuesday, April 11, was launching day at Story's and as the time of high water approached, several thousand people had gathered on every vantage point about the little river basin, and extra busses from Gloucester were bringing still more. This was to be the third cup contender launched in Essex in the past twelve months, and excitement throughout the region was running high. A small army of news photographers and movie cameramen were on hand to record the event.

At 10:20 A.M. all was ready and the men with the big crosscut saws took their places at the ends of the launching ways. On the starboard side were Willard Andrews and Bill Swett; on the port side it was Sammy Gray and Jake Story. At the signal from launching foreman Jack Doyle they sawed to the first two marks, then, pausing a moment, they all sawed like mad and with a resounding crack she was off. Miss Winnie L. Morrissey, the captain's daughter, smashed her bottle of wine and *Henry Ford* took the initial plunge. And quite a plunge it was—right into the mud bank on the opposite side of the river. The tugs *Eveleth* and *Lebanon H. Jenkins*, which had come to take her away, pulled for forty minutes to free her before being able to start for Gloucester. Once more, as had happened the year before with

Mayflower, the delay was sufficient to lose the tide, and *Henry Ford* was stuck, only this time it was out on the bar which makes across the mouth of the Essex River. Incredibly, both tugs left her, intending to come back the next day and get her off. Mother Nature, it seems, had other ideas, and at high water on the night tide *Henry Ford* floated free all by herself and was cast up on Coffin's Beach near Hawkes' Point, coming to rest right beside the ledges.

This, to put it mildly, was a hell of a situation. Here was a brand new $30,000 vessel on the beach and in imminent danger of breaking up. The wind had turned east and the surf was breaking almost over her. Try as they would, the *Eveleth* and the *Jenkins* and the big *Pallas* from Boston could not get her off. They did manage to slew her around some but in such a way that the night tide only moved her closer to the rocks. Fortunately she seemed to be standing the ordeal with no signs of serious hull damage, although portions of the shoe came ashore and she was taking quite a little water forward. The greatest fear was that the hull would be severely strained or even hogged, a condition impossible to correct.

Four days they worked. The *Lebanon Jenkins* was replaced by another big Boston tug, the *Neptune*, with the Coast Guard cutter *Ossipee* standing by a little off shore. On Thursday a wrecking lighter with a pontoon was brought over and the next day, in a supreme effort, the *Ford* was pulled from the beach. This triumph was short-lived since she promptly became stuck out on the bar again. Once more the tugs heaved mightily and on Saturday afternoon, at long last, the *Henry Ford* was freed. After anchoring back in the Essex River overnight, *Neptune*, with *Henry Ford* in tow, arrived at the Rocky Neck railways in Gloucester on Easter Sunday.

The next day she was hauled out for examination and repairs. Incredible as it seems, after all the abuse to which the hull had been subjected, she showed no signs of serious damage. A number of seams needed recaulking, three planks were replaced, the rudder stock repaired and several new pieces of shoe were put on the keel. The hull showed no sign of being hogged.

46

Completion of repairs and final settlement with the insurance company occasioned a delay of several weeks in outfitting for sea, so that it was the middle of May before the *Ford's* spars were stepped. In view of the circumstances, the Trustees of the international trophy waived the regulation requiring departure for the banks by April 30. Work was carried on with all possible haste, however, and by Friday, June 2, *Henry Ford* was ready to sail.

A tug had been ordered for 10:00 A.M. to pull *Henry Ford* from her berth at the wharf and down the harbor. At 10:00 A.M. the tug came and pulled—but *Henry Ford* wouldn't move. For the fifth time the vessel was stuck. Undismayed, Captain Morrissey said they'd wait until after dinner when the tide would be coming, so they did, and this time all was well. *Henry Ford* left on her maiden voyage that afternoon for a trip of salt fish.

As it had for *Puritan*, Gloucester gave the *Henry Ford* a rousing send-off with horns and whistles and crowds and the Lufkin and Tarr cannon. Captain Clayt had expressed gratitude to the Canadians for waiving the rules in his behalf and assured everyone he had no fears of sailing on his maiden trip on Friday, a circumstance of considerable concern to many at dockside for whom any Friday departure, whether maiden or otherwise, was an occasion to be avoided. Many fishermen (and skippers) felt strongly about this, to the point of not allowing a new vessel to be launched on Friday, and, beyond that, of not allowing the keel of the new vessel to be laid on Friday. (Moreover, one never turned a hatch cover bottom up, red mittens were not worn in the shipyard and a departing vessel must never be watched out of sight.)

With the international races scheduled to be held off Gloucester in the fall it was time for Gloucester to be about her preparations, and on August 1 the Gloucester committee chose William J. MacInnis as its chairman with William E. Parsons treasurer and Wilmot Reed, of *Mayflower* encounter fame, as secretary. As one of their first orders of business the committee began the arrangements for an elimination race to be held as before on October 12. (It had been reported that the winner of the Canadian elimination race was to be eligible for a $5,000 prize.) Applications were accepted from *Mayflower, L. A. Dunton* and *Yankee* of Boston and *Elizabeth Howard* and *Henry Ford* of Gloucester.

With announcement that *Mayflower* was accepted as an entrant, the old hassle regarding her qualifications began all over again. There was much sentiment in Canada as well as in Gloucester in support of *Mayflower*. It was claimed with considerable justification that she could hardly now be described as anything but a bona fide fisherman inasmuch as she had been fishing all through the preceding winter, and if that didn't make her a fisherman, what did? "Yacht lines" or not, she had proven herself, and *Mayflower's* owners felt that this time their boat was entitled to a fair consideration. It turned out that the Trustees felt otherwise and on September 14 voted a second time to bar *Mayflower*, supporting their action with a rather nebulous statement to the effect that she was a "fresh" fisherman and further taking exception to the amount of space in *Mayflower* taken up by permanent ballast. If further proof was needed that the Trustees were afraid of *Mayflower*, this was it. In later years Angus Walters himself was reported to have admitted as much.

In contradistinction to the action of the committee the previous year, the Gloucester committee this time went to bat for the *Mayflower* and did all they could to argue her case. They sent representatives to Halifax in company with designer Burgess in an attempt to demonstrate *Mayflower's* capacity and capabilities. The case seemed to hinge on whether *Mayflower* could carry as big a load as *Bluenose*, but in spite of the delegates' best efforts, the Trustees remained adamant, insisting that *Mayflower's* capacity was too small. At this, even many Canadians were outraged, and the suggestion was made that certain of the Trustees who were interested in *Bluenose* should resign and allow others to pass on *Mayflower's* elegibility. It was further suggested that maybe a substitute race should be held which would allow *Mayflower* to compete, an idea which was seconded by the American committee. "Let's have a free-for-all to decide the fastest schooner," they said, "and never mind the trophy this year." The point was, they wanted to see *Mayflower* in a race.

48

With monumental indifference to all the noise, the Trustees wired Gloucester on October 2 that it was hoped the plans for the international races would proceed as originally conceived. The Gloucester committee, with no choice, acceded to the dictum of the Trustees and ruled *Mayflower* ineligible for the elimination contest. Meanwhile, of course, arrangements of details were under way with an intensive campaign in progress among Gloucester citizens and businessmen to raise an expense and prize fund of $12,000. The *Henry Ford* had arrived on September 23 from her second trip salt banking and was now making preparations to race. Captain Morrissey was generous in praise of his new vessel, saying she showed well in all kinds of weather. (There had been a surge of apprehension during the summer when one of *Henry Ford*'s name boards was found floating at sea after having been accidentally ripped off.)

The owners of *Mayflower* were understandably vexed at being turned down a second time. There had been a considerable public clamor for a demonstration of the vessel's abilities, and the owners were extremely anxious to pit their schooner against others in a formal contest. They requested permission to sail in the eliminations anyway, to satisfy, as they said, the public's wish for a chance to see *Mayflower* in action. It was also suggested as an alternative proposal that just for sport she might challenge the winner of the elimination race. The committee decided, however, and probably with good judgment, that it would be unwise for *Mayflower* to compete even unofficially in the elimination race. They did suggest that perhaps she could challenge the winner of the international race when that event had been completed.

As preparations for the big events proceeded in Gloucester, the tension and excitement increased in inverse proportion to the amount of time remaining. Not since the appearance of Kipling's *Captains Courageous* had emotion run so high. The committee wished that people would get excited enough to contribute to the fund a little faster since with race day only a couple of weeks away they still had quite a sum to collect. The *Gloucester Times* did its bit to whip up enthusiasm and dutifully

49

printed the list of new contributors each day—even the twenty-five cent ones. Plans were made for social events, and invitations went out far and wide to dignitaries and notables. It was disappointing that President Harding had to send his regrets.

In preparation for racing, *Henry Ford* was hauled out on the railways on Monday, October 2. While there, she was officially measured and found to have a waterline length of 109.47 feet and a draft of 15.12 feet. Designer Tom McManus came down to inspect his newest creation. Elsewhere in Gloucester the *Elizabeth Howard* was also being made ready, and a couple of days later both boats were taken out for trial spins. Captain Morrissey and Tom McManus both seemed pleased with the *Ford's* performance and many critics felt that *Ford* was an exceptionally good vessel, some even going so far as to pronounce her the nearest thing to perfection that had ever been turned out in the shape of a fishing vessel.

Meanwhile at Halifax the Canadians were proceeding with their own elimination contest. The owners of *Bluenose* had somehow felt she should have been nominated as the defender without the formality of a series of races, but to this the Trustees said no; she would have to compete for the honor. A series for the best two out of three was begun on Saturday, October 7, with *Bluenose* an easy winner over *Canadia, Margaret K. Smith* and *Mahaska.* On Monday they went at it again, but with *Bluenose* so obviously superior to the others in all points of sailing, the officials did not wait for the finish to decide in her favor.

On Thursday, October 12, four vessels appeared at the starting line to try for the best two out of three in Gloucester's elimination series. From Boston had come *L. A. Dunton* with Capt. Felix Hogan and *Yankee* with Capt. Michael Brophy. The Gloucester boats were *Elizabeth Howard,* Capt. Ben Pine, and *Henry Ford,* Capt. Clayton Morrissey.

For a vessel which had been so highly vaunted before the race, the *Henry Ford* turned in a rather disappointing performance. She appeared logy and in rather poor trim and seemed at times to be slow in responding to her helm. For a time the *L. A. Dunton* and *Yankee* made it an interesting contest. The *Elizabeth*

50

Howard, a surprisingly fast vessel, suffered the misfortune which seemed to be common to racing when her main topmast carried away and she was forced to withdraw. The *Ford* did come on to win with a time of 5 hours, 31 minutes and 26 seconds for the forty-mile course, with *Yankee* 15 minutes, 53 seconds behind. A very poor third was *L. A. Dunton* coming 37 minutes behind the *Ford*.

Although the next race was scheduled for the following day, they waited until Saturday to allow time for *Elizabeth Howard* to make repairs. Saturday's race proved to be a better contest and although the *Ford* got off to a slow start, she seemed to come alive and perform more as expected. Captain Clayt had heeded the advice of Tom McManus and made ballast changes. He also had a couple of good amateur yachtsmen aboard. Ben Pine in his *Elizabeth Howard* made it a good race, though, and *Henry Ford's* winning margin over the *Howard* was only 5 minutes 20 seconds.

Some early risers, passing along the waterfront on Saturday morning, noted with interest that a strange schooner was lying at anchor out near Ten Pound Island. One of them did a quick double-take, realizing he was looking at none other than the *Bluenose*. Here was the city planning a gala welcome for their Canadian guest and without anyone realizing it, there she was, having slipped into the harbor in the wee hours of the morning. Nobody had planned on an eventuality of this kind, and it took a few frantic hurry-up phone calls and some scrambling around before the committee could get out there and extend a proper greeting. With a 7:30 A.M. departure from Halifax on Wednesday, it had been expected that *Bluenose* would arrive during the day on Friday, but a combination of fog and then gales made it heavy going—thus the delay. She had left Halifax in tow of the Canadian destroyer *Patriot* but with the bad weather had decided it was safer to go it alone. (From the vantage point of 1969 it seems unbelievable that, in 1922, communication between *Bluenose* and the towing *Patriot* was accomplished by passing a bottle along the 700 foot tow-line.)

With all preliminaries out of the way, the two contenders

devoted the next week to their preparations and tuning up for the featured event. People came from far and wide to look at the racers and speculate on their possibilities. *Mayflower's* owners were determined to see their vessel in a race, and early in the week made arrangements with both contenders for *Mayflower* to meet the trophy winner at the conclusion of the series. The *Boston Herald,* in an editorial, commented on the emotions and high hopes of all New England for victory by *Henry Ford.* For its part, the *Boston Transcript* noted the woeful lack of hotel accommodations in Gloucester for all who wanted to come. The *Bluenose* was hauled out for measurement and found to have a waterline length of 111.80 feet and a draft of 15.66 feet. Her sail area was figured at 9,771 square feet. Betting odds shifted from even money to five to four on *Henry Ford.* All appeared to be ready for the start of Saturday's race—but was it?

On Friday afternoon it was announced by the International Race Committee that *Henry Ford's* sail area was greater than that allowed under the Deed of Gift, which said that all sail area must not exceed 80% of the square of the waterline length expressed in square feet. With a waterline length of 109.47, that would mean that *Ford* was entitled to 9,587.1 square feet of sail, and as far as Clayt and his men knew, *Henry Ford* was within the limits. The official measurer appointed by the committee, a man from "Boston Tech," said otherwise. Rather than under, *Ford* was 437 feet over the limit, he said, and the sails must be cut.

This was indeed a blow to Captain Morrissey, but there seemed to be no arguing with the committee, so off came the mainsail and it was rushed up to Marion Cooney's United Sail Loft to have two whole cloths removed from the leach. They took the fore gaff topsail off too, planning to remove two and a half cloths from that. With a thoughtfully provided supply of prescription whiskey to bolster their efforts, the sailmakers worked all night, finishing barely in time to get the sails back aboard for the 10:00 A.M. start. In a less controversial decision, the committee voted to allow President Harding's representative, Secretary of the Navy Edwin Denby, to sail as a passenger on the *Ford.*

Nip and tuck though it was, the *Ford* came out to meet her rival at the line and at ten o'clock both vessels were off—or so they thought. Actually a postponement signal was run up the pole of the committee boat, it being felt that there wasn't wind enough just then. Neither skipper, however, paid any attention to it and so after ten minutes a recall signal was sent up. Again the signal was ignored and the schooners sailed on. At 10:30 the committee sent a motorboat alongside the leading *Henry Ford* with a request for the vessels to turn back, but Captain Morrissey wasn't about to take orders from a yachtsman in a motorboat. Inasmuch as both vessels were determined to carry on, the committee gave up its attempts to stop them and their boat proceeded to the successive marks to note the times of passing. The *Henry Ford*, proving herself a good vessel in light airs, established a commanding lead and held it over the entire course, leading *Bluenose* at the finish by nearly a mile. The trouble was that at the finish line no committee boat was there to acknowledge the result. With the rounding of the third mark by the contestants, the committee had decided to call it a day and head for home. But committee or no committee, the schooners had raced, both vessels had finished within the time limit, and *Henry Ford* had won. Captain Walters readily conceded an honorable defeat at the hands of Captain Morrissey, announcing to one and all that he had been beaten fairly and squarely. Moreover, he declared that if the *Ford* beat him again, he would go fishing and leave the cup in Gloucester.

The actions of the committee were hard to understand. Apparently realizing that a most difficult situation would ensue if the race was carried through and completed after having been signalled to stop, and realizing further that by appearing at the first three marks they had tacitly condoned what was going on, they gambled that the wind, which was then dying out almost completely, would solve the problem for them by making it impossible for the schooners to complete the course in time, thereby automatically making it "no race." However, they lost their gamble, and instead of a dead beat to the finish in failing airs, the wind shifted and sprang up, making a comfortable reach to line.

53

No doubt a victory served in some measure to assuage Captain Morrissey's feelings regarding his cut mainsail, but any jubilation he may have experienced was very short-lived. The committee went into session and announced two things: first, that, because of the false start, the contest would be declared "no race"; second, that the official measurer had made a mistake in his calculations and the *Henry Ford's* mainsail was still too big and must be cut again! If it hadn't dawned on the fishermen before, it certainly did now that they were sailing in a yacht race, not a fishermen's contest. What a far cry all this was from the great days of "the race it blew" or, yes, even the contest of *Esperanto* and *Delawana*.

With the greatest reluctance, Captain Clayt once more took off the mainsail and back it went to the sail loft to be cut again. This time they took out another fifty-seven square feet. The measurer had acknowledged his error on Saturday just before the race when obviously there was no time to do anything about it, so that had nothing else happened, the race would still have been no contest.

With no race scheduled for Sunday, Captain Morrissey and his men had time to reflect upon their situation and the more they thought about it, the madder they got. By Monday morning they had about made up their minds that they wanted no more of this racing business. Mrs. Pauline Raymond, wife of one of *Ford's* owners, Jonathan Raymond, and no less a person than Navy Secretary Denby pleaded with Captain Clayt for the honor of Gloucester and the United States. At length he relented, saying to the crew, "Come on, boys. Let's go today. Get the mainsail on and let's get started." They asked for a one hour postponement but the committee refused, having said that adherence to the rules was a matter of law; they could not allow fishermen to take over the conduct of the races themselves. As if to heap a few more coals onto the fires of controversy, Captain Walters had himself refused to go out unless the American observer on his boat was changed and a man of his own choosing put aboard the *Ford*.

With minutes to spare, the *Ford* arrived at the line where *Blue-*

nose was waiting. That she got there at all was something of a minor triumph, since quite a number of the crew had actually quit in disgust, and Captain Morrissey was obliged to gather some hasty replacements; all this added to the work of bending on the mainsail again. At ten o'clock he crossed the line and squared away but *Bluenose* stayed where she was. At this point a one hour postponement signal was run up and Captain Morrissey was forced to turn back. They both started at eleven, with *Bluenose* first over the line. She was soon overhauled by the *Ford,* which took the lead and held it, coming on to win by 2 minutes 26 seconds, in spite of having a makeshift crew and a monstrously ill-fitting mainsail. In this race the *Ford* had demonstrated a superiority over *Bluenose* in reaching and going to windward in light air and smooth sea. While out on the course they had met the "phantom racer" *Mayflower,* who again showed a speed on the first two legs much superior to either of the contestants under the prevailing conditions.

With *Henry Ford* back at the wharf and tied up for the night, Captain Morrissey came ashore and announced that as far as he was concerned, he had won two races and the series was over. He gave orders to begin taking out the ballast in the morning and to prepare for fishing, saying there was nothing to be gained by sailing another race. When asked about a possible sacrifice of prize money he replied: "It has cost me and my men enough already so that the matter of a few thousand dollars does not count against the principle involved." (The winner of the series was to get $3,000 and the loser $2,000.)

What was supposed to have been a gala banquet was held in Gloucester's state armory that night in honor of the competing crews. There was little gaiety, however, what with affairs mixed up worse than a Chinese fire drill and Captain Clayt refusing to race any more. It developed that contrary to the announced intentions of the Canadians to turn over the cup if the *Ford* won a second race, they now desired to continue the series. In effect they renounced their original willingness to let the first race stand. By so doing it was widely felt that the men of Nova Scotia passed up what might have been a magnificent gesture of sportsmanship. Remarked someone: "They could have gone home heroes." Like a wet firecracker, the whole affair was fizzling out.

True to his word, Captain Clayt began Tuesday morning preparations to resume fishing. Frantic behind-the-scenes efforts of the night before while the banquet was in progress had been to no avail. Officially the day's race was postponed on the representation that Captain Morrissey was sick. When asked about it, he agreed he wasn't feeling well but said that mostly he was "sick of committees and yachting rules and this and that and other things which spoiled the sport we set out on."

Tuesday evening, in a last-ditch effort to get him to change his mind, Mr. and Mrs. Raymond invited Captain Morrissey and his men to their home for a private dinner. Their entreaties must have been successful, for the captain agreed to go on and finish the series, the crew consenting to go down to the wharf early in the morning and start putting the ballast back aboard. This they did in a pouring rain, for it stormed the next day with a fairly strong wind. Mr. Silver of the Trustees came down to the wharf to oversee the operation and make sure the ballast went back as it had been before. It wasn't pleasant to work in the rain and wet sails would be more difficult to handle. It had been noted that *Bluenose* kept a set of covers on her sails whenever she was tied up, a luxury of equipment not possessed by the Gloucestermen, who wondered what a fishing vessel was doing with a set of sail covers.

To give *Henry Ford* time to finish preparations, the start of Wednesday's race was postponed to 11:00 A.M. In the maneuvering for the start following the five-minute gun, the *Ford* at one point came within a whisker of sailing aboard the *Bluenose* when the latter, running dead off the wind, refused to give way to the *Ford* (then on a starboard tack) as sailing rules required. The sailing committee ignored it although competent observers were emphatic in stating that *Bluenose* should immediately have been disqualified. Although the *Ford* was first over the line and leading briefly, *Bluenose* this time overhauled her and led for the rest of the way, winning by a comfortable margin. It was obvious that

Ford was greatly handicapped by her mainsail, which was now reduced in size and ruined in fit.

On Thursday in a good breeze of wind it was do or die for *Henry Ford,* and she died. Though seemingly outclassed in a real thresh to windward she was making a race of it, showing well on the reaches and proving to be about equal down wind, but then it happened—she lost her fore topmast and that was the end. As he had the year before, Angus dowsed his fore topsail so as not to hold an unfair advantage. With a good lead, *Bluenose* went on to win. The series was over at last; or maybe we should say the sailing was over, but the words, the charges and the counter-charges were far from over.

Perhaps it would be in order at this point to pause briefly and explain the committee structure which governed the international races. First were the nine Trustees of the trophy, all Canadians, in whose custody the trophy lay and who reserved to themselves the administration and interpretation of and changes in the terms and regulations of the Deed of Gift. Next came the International Race Committee, an agency of the Trustees and committee of five, whose membership was divided between the two countries, and whose job was to oversee the general conduct and management of the races and who in turn appointed a five member International Sailing Committee. This was the group which actually ran the races and governed the sailing. It was they who established the sailing regulations and rules of the road and then supervised a proper adherence to the same, and it was they who in this series were the center of all the storms of controversy. Lastly was the American (or Canadian) Race Committee which, one might say, was the representative of the home town and was the one which really did all the work. It was their job to attend to all the details incidental to holding a race (or races), to select the competitors, and most important of all, to assume responsibility for raising the necessary funds.

Though more or less quietly busy in the background through the tumultuous days of the past week, the American Race Committee, loyal Gloucestermen all under the leadership of William J. MacInnis, had been doing all they could to smooth the path

57

of progress and to insure fair and equitable treatment for the Gloucester boat. They had been doing a little "inspecting and measuring" of their own and as a result felt it incumbent upon themselves to come forward at this point and lodge a series of protests with the International Race Committee, charging *Bluenose* and Captain Walters with four violations of the provisions of the Deed of Gift, to wit:

1. That Captain Walters failed to report the absence of an American observer aboard the *Bluenose* during the third and fourth races.

2. That ballast aboard the *Bluenose* was shifted during the series and also during individual races.

3. That a fisherman's staysail of improper size was substituted for the regular staysail on *Bluenose*.

4. That the texture and quality of *Bluenose*'s sails was not that of "ordinary commercial duck commonly used by fishermen."

In connection with the first point it should be stated that under the rules, each vessel was required to carry an observer representing the other side, presumably to insure fair play. Captain Walters had objected to the American man on his boat and wished for a replacement, so arrangements were made to change observers. For some reason this new man misunderstood the directions given him and never appeared aboard *Bluenose*. Therefore, according to proper procedure, it was the duty of Captain Walters to notify the sailing committee that he had no American observer.

The second charge arose from observation of certain furtive nocturnal activities involving ballast on board the *Bluenose*, plus miscellaneous reports from "informed sources." What appeared to be ballast thrown from the *Bluenose* showed in the dock at low tide.

Point number three arose, shall we say, from simple observation, also point number four. It had been noted that *Bluenose*'s working sails came off upon arrival in Gloucester and were stored in a rented garage. The sails she carried in the races were obviously of finer quality and were kept under covers. It was the general belief that these racing sails were of English duck.

The International Race Committee, which itself had been subject to upheaval when two of the original American members resigned, received the protests and took them under advisement. The protests notwithstanding, it was planned to wind up the affairs of an incredible week on Friday noon with a presentation and farewell lunch for Captain Walters and his crew, the event to be the time of formally awarding the trophy and prize money. In a circumstance almost beyond belief, the body of one of *Bluenose's* crewmen was found on Friday morning floating in the dock where he had evidently fallen and drowned the night before. When the men of the *Bluenose* gathered for the luncheon, it seemed difficult to understand why they were there. The skipper was away attending to the melancholy affair of the lost shipmate and there seemed nothing to be joyful about; with all of the bitterness engendered by the disputes and contretemps of the past week, their ultimate win over *Henry Ford* had proved something of a Pyrrhic victory; and now with protests lodged with the International Race Committee the awarding of prizes was held up pending the outcome of the necessary investigation. So, in effect, the guests ate and left. That afternoon, with her flag at half mast and the crew in silence, the *Bluenose,* under the command of the mate, sailed for Lunenburg. The Race Committee, after deliberations that afternoon and evening, finally reached a decision and announced on Saturday morning that the protests of the *Henry Ford* were disallowed. The first prize of $3,000 would be sent to *Bluenose.*

In a situation somewhat analogous to the final bomb in a fireworks display, Captain Larkin of the *Mayflower* appeared in town on Friday afternoon to conclude arrangements for the promised race between *Bluenose* and himself. Captain Walters had indicated the day before that he would race the *Mayflower* off Boston and Captain Larkin had been attending to details. On finding the *Bluenose* gone, he was, as they said, fit to be tied.

Thus ended a week in the annals of fishermen's racing and in the history of Gloucester the like of which could hardly have been imagined. All the anticipation and expectation of a glorious holiday period in the life of the city, with its hopes of thrilling victory for the pride of the local fleet, had slipped away and vanished in a fiasco of awesome proportions. It was like a bad dream. For Captain Morrissey the events of each day seemed almost in league to exacerbate the difficulties of the day before. It was generally agreed, however, that he emerged from it all a giant of character and sportsmanship. As a kind of postscript and as one bright spot in an otherwise dismal period, a group of his friends banded together and conducted a campaign for funds to buy him a new mainsail. To this, Gloucester subscribed with a will. In another gesture of friendliness a Boston newspaper presented the captain with a specially inscribed loving cup in appreciation of his sportsmanship. Come to think of it, perhaps Captain Morrissey shouldn't have left on that maiden trip on a Friday.

4 ★ Columbia

With the defeat of his *Elizabeth Howard* in the elimination races of October 1922, Ben Pine perforce became an interested spectator of the events which followed. He could sympathize with Clayt Morrissey's desire to have nothing more to do with racing, but Ben had a demonstrated ability to handle a schooner under racing conditions and felt he would like to have another new vessel to replace the *Puritan* and try his own luck in a competition with the *Bluenose*. This talent of his for handling a schooner must have been something of a gift, since he had never had any experience as a fishing skipper. Coming from his native Newfoundland in 1893 at the age of ten, he had gone fishing for a few years as a young man, later turning to a sort of trading business with partner Joseph Langsford, dealing originally in old sails and ship's hardware. They began to buy shares of vessels, and in 1922 along with several others formed the Atlantic Supply Co., a firm of ship chandlers and vessel operators, chartering and managing quite a number of smaller schooners.

With this great desire to have another vessel and race the *Bluenose,* Ben had already approached Starling Burgess for a set of plans, and with the end of the season's racing he went about the task of organizing a group of backers. A nucleus for this group was enlisted from the Manta Club in Kenneth Ferguson and Marion Cooney, who, with Ben Pine, formed the original proprietorship of the new Columbia Associates, Inc. Shares were to be offered to the public at $100 apiece. From their name, it was obvious they planned to call their schooner *Columbia.*

At first they considered using *Puritan's* lines again, but in light of recent experience and with newly announced modifications of the Deed of Gift in mind, it was decided to evolve a completely new design. A winning combination, they hoped, might at last

61

come from the experience and skill of one of the country's great designers.

Mention of modifications in the Deed of Gift points up the fact that the rules were indeed becoming more elaborate, to the extent that one wonders if the international races were not about to become in reality nothing more nor less than yachting contests with the fishermen as seemingly innocent pawns in a situation that appeared to be beyond their influence. We now find provisions for minimum displacement, maximum length and maximum sparring, designed, the Trustees said, to provide a vessel of a type suitable for the fishing industry and of commercial value to the exclusion of racing machines. None of the modifications, however, would be applicable to *Bluenose* as an existing vessel. Meanwhile, in Lunenburg, Angus Walters was proposing an ocean race between his *Bluenose* and the *Mayflower*. The race was to be sailed from Newfoundland to the West Indies and return, with cargoes both ways, for a side bet of $10,000.

By mid-November, *Columbia's* plans were ready and an agreement to build the vessel was reached with Arthur D. Story in Essex, the town that had produced each of the other American racing schooners. This fact of itself was especially noteworthy as Gloucester men had been having their ships built in Essex for close to 200 years. By the time the Columbia Associates got there, upwards of 3,000 vessels had come from Essex yards. The building of these wooden ships in Essex, Massachusetts, had been the dominant industry of the little town since the 1660s, when, as Chebacco parish in the town of Ipswich, a riverside tract was set apart by the colonial legislature as common land to be used by the inhabitants for the building of ships. This industry reached the point where in 1852 there were no less than fifteen shipyards in town and the products of these builders were to become known the world over. The Essex yards worked closely with the fishermen to create advancements and improvements in design and rig. Several notable changes in hull form initiated by Essex builders achieved wide recognition and acceptance in the fishing industry of the whole region.

Over the years an intimate maritime and business relationship had grown between the neighboring communities of Gloucester and Essex. As Gloucester grew and developed as a fishing port of importance, its fishermen became Essex' best customers. To quote a few brief statistics, the record shows that in 1922, the year of our story, the Gloucester registry listed 177 vessels of all sizes of which 72 had been built in Essex. Back in the all-sail days of 1880 the proportion was even higher, with 218 of Gloucester's fleet of 475 schooners, sloops and other boats having been built in Essex. Besides actually building the boats, the Essex builders cooperated in and assisted the development of the industry by providing much of the financing which made the vessel construction possible. They did this in several ways: by adopting the practice of spreading payment for their work over a period of years following a vessel's completion; by deferring at least until after launching the requirement for any substantial sum; by taking a share of the vessel and/or a mortgage for much of the cost. In the case of the new *Columbia,* this practice was carried on with Arthur D. Story, the builder, taking a substantial mortgage on the vessel. The year before, he had bought a share of the *Henry Ford.*

The conclusion of an agreement between Columbia Associates, Inc., and Mr. Story set into motion the actual construction of the ship. Though expected to become a contender for the Dennis Trophy, *Columbia* was still to be essentially a working fisherman which must pay her own way. She was to be built with types and methods of construction typical of hundreds of her sisters in Canada as well as the United States. In 1922 the actual building processes of a wooden fishing vessel were substantially the same as those in use for generations, and the men who carried them on were frequently descendants of long lines of shipwrights. Advancing developments of communication and transportation had not as yet wholly dissolved the relative isolation of small New England towns, and the folkways and industries of these little places often remained much as they had been for decades past. This was especially true in Essex where the rather unique nature of shipbuilding had involved much of the life of the town not only in the shipyards themselves but in numerous subsidiary industries. There were blacksmith shops which made the ironwork for spars and rigging; there were spar yards which made the masts and spars; there were shops for making tackle blocks, wooden pumps, windlasses and cabin finish work; and there were ropewalks which made the steam-tarred trawl lines used by the fishermen. Let us then visit Essex and the Story shipyard and watch construction of the new *Columbia,* A. D. Story's 354th hull.

It will be remembered that in the construction of vessels to compete for the trophy, time was of the essence, since in order to be eligible for competition in a given year a vessel must have left her last port of call for the banks by April 30. Therefore, with the calendar reminding him that it was late November and having Starling Burgess' plans at hand, it is quite probable that A. D. Story had gotten things underway without waiting for any formalities of signing a contract; word-of-mouth agreements had always been honored in Essex. As a matter of fact this particular job had come to Essex at a very opportune time inasmuch as new building had been at a virtual standstill since late July. For work there had been only Story's big three-master the *Adams,* begun on speculation in the fall of 1920, and later, the little schooner *Marjorie Parker,* begun in November. Across the river the James yard had been temporarily shut down.

After examining the construction drawings to see if any timber was needed that he didn't already have up in the timber piles, A. D. Story took the lines over to Archer B. Poland's mold loft in South Essex where Archie would delineate the ship full size upon the lofting floor. From these lines he would make his templates of every piece. From long experience as the loftsman for each of the Essex yards, Archie knew what molds (Essex yards referred to templates as molds) would be needed first so that as soon as a few were done he would send them over.

Back in the yard the molds were immediately taken by A. D.'s younger brother, Edwin James Story, up to the slope behind the yard, where piles of timbers of every size and shape were spread over the ground. Carefully selecting suitable pieces, Eddie James traced out and marked the various members and rolled them out where Sammy Gray could hook onto them with "Red-eye," the old shipyard horse, and drag them to the mill. This weather-beaten lean-to structure housed what meager machinery the yard used. Centrally located inside was the large bricked-in boiler formerly used to power a band saw but now relegated to supplying the steam to the steaming box. To the right of the boiler was a space which seemed to be filled with large wooden pulleys and long flapping leather drive belts. These belts were driving first of all the thirty-eight inch band saw out in front and the grind stone and trunnel lathe inside. Motive power for all this was a single large electric motor which ran all day long. To the left of the boiler, in a kind of dim and sooty room, was a catch-all space for stuff which didn't seem to belong anywhere else, and also a bench in front of the window where Lib filed his saws. Lib, or more properly Liboire D'Entremont, was the sawyer and lord of this domain. People had forgotten how many years he had worked there but it had been a long time. Few men ever lived who worked any harder than Lib did. He was too crotchety for anyone to work with him so he did most of the sawing alone, wrestling hundreds of thousands of feet of oak timbers through the old band saw. He literally wore out two iron saw tables and once, after falling while carrying a timber, worked for two days with a broken arm before discovering what was wrong. He lived alongside the yard and would come to work seemingly at the crack of dawn to get his saws filed and catch up on any sawing he hadn't been able to finish the night before. Perhaps Lib's most memorable characteristic was his cleft palate, which made him sound as though he had a mouthful of mashed potatoes. This, coupled with a strong French Canadian accent and an ever present cigar, took some getting used to.

With the roughing out of the keel pieces and a start on the frame timbers, actual construction of *Columbia* got under way the week of Monday, December 4. It had been a pleasant and very dry fall to the point where people's cisterns and many wells were going dry. For a small town with no public water supply, this was a matter of some concern. However, it seemed that as soon as the work began on *Columbia* the weather took a turn for the worse and stayed that way. It rained on Tuesday, December 5, became very cold on Wednesday, and on Friday came the winter's first snowstorm. From that time on it seemed that storm piled on top of storm, each to be followed by a fresh onslaught of severe cold weather. In those days winter work out-of-doors in the shipyard could be a cruel and punishing proposition, but what else could a man do if that was his trade, and each lost hour reduced the already modest pay envelope by that much more? In a year that had seen a great deal of slack time, it was doubly important to stay on the job. But presumably a person can get used to nearly anything, and almost without exception every man in Story's gang had been doing this for a good many years.

The following week the big keel timbers were strung out, scarfed together and bolted, and on Saturday, December 16, the new keel was "turned up." To explain briefly, for the sake of convenience it was the custom to assemble a keel structure upside down. Then, when finished, the whole gang would grab it and bodily roll it over right side up. At that point it would be given its proper alignment and degree of declivity and placed upon the blocks and cribbing which would support the growing ship until the time of launching. This operation marked the first milestone, as it were, in the vessel's construction and often was the point at which a payment was due.

The Gloucester waterfront was already beginning to follow *Columbia*'s progress and we note that many subscriptions for shares were being received. In Canada, William Duff, M. P. for Lunenburg County, Nova Scotia, was voicing strong criticism of the rulings made by the Trustees of the trophy concerning displacement and spar dimensions, reflecting a growing dismay in both countries at trends in the conduct of the international races. A recent editorial of the respected *Boston Transcript* had suggested that "future races be conducted along the requirements of fishing rather than yachting."

In Essex, most people were not particularly concerned with questions like this. It was enough to do to build the vessels, earn

66

a living and carry on the life of home and town amid the worsening winter weather. We read in the newspapers of the day that, in spite of the recent storms, the Ladies' Home Circle held a very successful Christmas sale in the vestry of the Congregational Church and the supper and dance put on by the Pythian Sisters in the town hall drew a good attendance. The coming of the cold weather, however, forced a halt in the work of dredging the Essex River, with the job finished only up as far as Eben's Creek. By the week before Christmas, old John Hubbard, Malcolm MacIver and the others were "framing out" *Columbia* although the weather was hampering progress. It was announced that the vessel would be fitted for dory handlining under the command of Capt. Alden Geele.

In 1922, December was still a recognizable month in its own right, not yet having been submerged in the commercially sponsored Christmas orgies of years to come, so that it was perfectly natural for the people of Essex to hold a special town meeting on Saturday night, December 23. It seems that the police department had overrun its appropriation by $800 and wished a vote of the town to cover the overdue bills. Moreover, they wanted a supplemental appropriation of $500 to "clean out the joints in town and enforce the law." Gathering in the town hall, the voters chose George Mears to be the moderator and then listened as Caleb Cogswell, chairman of the board of selectmen and chief of police by virtue of his office, made the motion. At that point Lyman James, Ezra Hinckley and others rose and severely scored Chief Cogswell and Constable Stewart Hadley for their laxity in "allowing bootlegging and other lawlessness to become rampant in town." Furthermore, it was loudly charged that Essex was becoming "a resort for those outside the town who wish to avoid the law." At length Chief Cogswell got his $800 for the back bills, but the $500 Christmas bonus for the police department, as it was termed, was resoundingly voted down. The spirit of "goodwill towards men" presumably regained the upper hand the next day, for Christmas Sunday found all four Essex churches well attended with many visitors home for the holidays.

In the shipyard it was getting to be rather tough going. A new blizzard struck on Friday, December 29, and the evening trains into Essex and to Gloucester were running up to three hours late. The *Gloucester Daily Times* reported that seven Gloucester schooners were frozen in at Bay of Islands, Newfoundland. On Thursday, January 4, another blizzard hit Cape Ann and the following week was almost one continuous snow storm. In spite of all this the men at Story's erected first *Columbia*'s "square" frames, then the stem, the forward "cants," the stern structure, the transom and finally the after "cants." (In addition they were finishing the planking and starting the deck framing of the *Marjorie Parker*.) By way of explanation, the terms "square frames" and "cants" refer to those members of a vessel's structure more commonly known as "ribs." Through the central part of the ship each rib or frame is one continuous member from side to side. At the extremities of the ship, where the shape is finer, the frames are put up in halves, one on each side, and are called "cants." Each, whether square frame or cant, is a laminated member made up of two layers of heavy oak timbers sawed to the proper shape and bolted or trunneled together. In the case of *Columbia*, each layer of timber was six inches thick, so that a completed frame had a total thickness of twelve inches. Frames and cants were spaced twenty-four inches on centers. In a length of 140 feet, *Columbia* had sixty-three frames. With a typical square frame composed of eighteen members, it represented a lot of pieces, all of which had been sawed out by Liboire D'Entremont.

It was the custom at that time in the yards of Essex and in most local places of business to work six full days a week (with no coffee breaks). In fact, New Year's Day of 1923 was just another work day, although the majority of the gang managed to show up for only about five hours. It can be seen therefore that, with a 48 hour week and a gang of willing and able men, work on the *Columbia* would progress rapidly even with weather which was almost unbelievable for its severity. The snowbanks were piled high along the streets and sidewalks, and in the shipyard the berth where *Columbia* stood gradually took on the appearance of a great snow-lined trench. Each man was expected to have a shovel or a broom as part of his tool kit and before starting in the morning each man was further expected to use his shovel or broom to clear away the job he was doing. Moreover, he did this on his own time. On days of inclement weather each man used his own judgment as to whether he worked or not, generally, of course, working if it was at all possible to do so.

Sunday, January 7, in spite of the storm, there was a good attendance at the Congregational Church. Soprano Helen MacIver, Malcolm's daughter, sang two fine solos. That week the ladies of the sewing circle of the Catholic Church were entertained by Mrs. D'Entremont and the prizes at the weekly whist party held in Ezra Hinckley's barber shop were won by Madeline Boutchie, Carl Carter and Mr. Hinckley himself. It was announced by the school board that parents should judge for themselves whether to send their children to school on stormy days. If less than 50% of the pupils were present, no attendance would be recorded. "It's an ill wind that doesn't blow some good," however, as we note that Charlie Mears was ready to harvest a good crop of ice from Chebacco Lake and the ice on the Essex River now carried the huts of scores of smelt fishermen.

On Thursday, January 18, the *Gloucester Times* carried an item to the effect that the crew of the schooner *Mayflower*, tied up in Boston, had all quit after the owners, Mayflower Associates, had been unable to pay each man $100 for time lost in preparing the vessel for racing. Alone among his men, Capt. Henry Larkin had remained with the vessel, which would now have to be decommissioned. In Chester Basin, Nova Scotia, work was progressing on a new Canadian schooner expected to be a racer, although there, too, the weather was interfering with the work. At sea it was reported great ice fields were covering the Grand Banks, while in Gloucester the whole inner harbor was rapidly freezing over. Ben Pine's *Elizabeth Howard*, laden with tons of frozen spray, barely made it back to port with bad leaks and topside damage after battles with the storms. Four of her crew had been swept to their deaths.

As if the weather alone were not bad enough, the problems of people in this area were rapidly being compounded by a growing shortage of coal. The long coal strike of 1922 coupled with the

69

extremes of weather were rapidly reducing coal supplies to the vanishing point. It was indeed fast becoming a winter to remember.

On Friday, January 19, 1923, with the structural framework of the hull virtually complete, it was time for Willard Andrews, Harry Swett, Mark Hubbard, Jack Murphy and "Mac" MacIver to commence hanging plank. *Columbia* would now start to become a real vessel. The shaping and fitting of the planks to the frames of a vessel was one of the major processes involved in wooden shipbuilding. The planks formed the outer skin or shell of the ship and they alone separated the crew and cargo from the briny deep. Obviously, then, it took skill, workmanship and experience to prepare and fasten them on properly, and it took the concerted efforts of a good share of the gang to do it. Before Willard Andrews and his crew could "hang up" a plank on the side of the ship, it must first of all have been "lined out" or delineated upon a piece of rough stock. It was then taken to the mill and sawed out in the band saw. From the band saw it went to the bevellers who trimmed or bevelled the edges along the whole length of it so that it would lie snugly against the planks adjacent to it. Lastly the planking crew could take it from the bevellers and put it (or "hang" it) onto the ship.

It is reasonable to say that the most critical of these steps was the first one, the lining process, performed in this case by George Weston. How easily and how quickly the plankers accomplished their job reflected in a large measure how well George Weston had done his. This process of itself required skill and was composed of several steps. It began with George laying out with chalkline and rule how the plank was going to lie against the frames. He had to see that his intended edges were going to be good fair lines; he had to make sure the plank would not be unworkably wide or narrow; he had to decide where each plank was to be cut, keeping in mind what he had to work with for stock and also that proper distribution of joints and butts was vital to the strength of the completed structure; he had to decide approximately how many strips or "streaks" of planking the finished boat would ultimately have, and then be careful to divide the girth of the boat at its various points so that it would all come out right, with the top edge of the ship not too high or too low at any given spot. You see, the number of streaks remained the same from bow to stern, yet the girth of the boat changed tremendously from midships to either end. Moreover, he had to take into account the long sloping rake of the stem and the great depth of the ship in the vicinity of the rudder. With all of these conditions to observe, he had to work fast enough to keep ahead of the plankers.

While George Weston was going about his work of laying out the planks, old John Hubbard was going around and around the boat dubbing the frames in preparation for receiving the planks. "To dub" meant to trim each frame with an adze so that the plank would lie firmly and smoothly against it. The frames, as they were erected by the framers, were merely close approximations of their eventual exact shape, the final shaping and trimming being done by the dubber who, each time he went around the boat, dubbed a spot equal in width to the plank which would lie there. It might be interjected here that much of the success of a planking job was also attributable to the dubber, whose skill or lack of it made a big difference in the time it took to hang a plank. John Hubbard was a master of this skill, who took the trouble to check the work the plankers were doing as he went along. Occasionally finding a spot where the plank was not completely snugged up to a frame, he would grab a maul or a beetle and fetch the plank a mighty belt, growling as he did so, "What's da use to dub?"

John Hubbard, like Lib, was no Sunny Jim as far as disposition was concerned, but being a dubber he too was able to do much of his work alone. Inevitably he was the occasional target of the practical jokers in the yard, chief of whom was Sammy Gray. Sammy was an ebullient and irrepressible character whose job was to care for and guide the shipyard horse in dragging the timbers about the yard, to help Lib in sawing timbers too hard for him to handle alone and in between times to putty and paint or perform any job which was not within the province of any other man. It was the custom for many of the men, including

71

John Hubbard, to take home a basket of big chips every night for the kitchen stove. One day as he passed by, Sammy noticed John's basket filled with chips sitting by the bow of the boat. With a grin of inspiration he disappeared, shortly to return lugging a length of heavy chain. Removing the chips he placed the chain in the bottom of the basket, then covering it over carefully with a layer of fresh chips, he eagerly awaited the result. Four o'clock, and John started for his basket. Grabbing the handle, he whirled around in a semi-circle and fell to the ground, much to the delight of a large group of concealed onlookers.

It is safe to say that the work of the plankers was about the most laborious of any of the jobs in the shipyard. On *Columbia*, for example, the planks were long-leaf yellow pine and oak, both of which are among the heaviest of woods. Each plank finished 2¾ inches thick and might average about 9 or 10 inches wide. Individual planks would range up to thirty feet long or more. In planking a vessel it was customary to cover the lower part of the hull with the yellow pine and to use oak along the upper streaks where the degree of abrasion was higher. As soon as the bevellers had finished trimming the edges of a plank, the shout "Hang 'em up!" rang out as the planking crew came to lug it up to the working stage. Usually the bevellers helped them do this and anyone else in the area was also expected to help. If a plank was one which required a lot of twisting, it had first to go to the steam box where it reposed until sufficiently pliable. Having arrived on the staging, the plank was lifted into place (or "hung") and seized with huge iron C-clamps. It would then be clamped and wedged snugly against its neighbors and "spiked off," which means that just enough iron spikes would be put into it to keep it from falling down; the butt was cut and the plankers moved on to the next one. Coming along now behind the plankers would be the fastener, Frank White Story, who bored the holes and drove the treenail or "trunnel" fastenings. Trunnels were the locust pegs 1⅛ or 1¼ inches in diameter which held the planks on. We might add that with two of these holes to be bored at every frame and with four in way of butts, and with a trunnel to be turned on the lathe and driven into each, Frank White

72

couldn't exactly let any grass grow under his feet. Let it be said that in an average day, a good planking crew would apply from two to two and a half streaks of planking or, in other words, would work themselves around the boat two and one half times. *Columbia* had twenty-three streaks fastened with approximately 13,000 trunnels.

Planking the outside of the vessel was really only little more than half the battle, for the inside had to be planked too. This job was started by a second crew when the outside was about one-half or two-thirds done. The operation was not as fussy as the outside since it was not necessary to achieve water-tight seams and exact fit was not as important. Furthermore, the inside planking did not extend all the way down to the keel. Inside planks were referred to as "ceiling." (Whether "ceiling" or "sealing" has always been a debatable point. In Essex it was "ceiling.")

The coming of February brought no change as far as the weather was concerned. If anything, it got worse. Through January there had been thirteen days when severity of weather had caused some loss of time in the shipyard, and on five of those days there had been no work at all. In February there were to be another eleven days including five more in which nobody worked. But weather or not, things were active in Essex. Best of all, the James yard was busy again building two schooner yachts, the *Isabel Q.* and the *Wanderer*; a political campaign was beginning to heat up with young Bill Wyeth challenging a trio of old-timers, Frank McKenzie, Aaron Cogswell and John P. Story, for the office of selectman, and for school board a lively scrap was developing between Parker Choate and Alden Burnham. Malcolm MacIver and Ben Lander were challenging Stewart Hadley for constable. At the Town Hall, rehearsals were getting under way for the annual veteran firemen's minstrel show. John "Shine" Wilson was chairman of the committee. (We might add that John Wilson later starred in the show.) The scarcity of coal, however, forced the school board to add an extra five days to the regular winter recess.

And still it snowed! With a snow plow coming down ahead of

it, the 7.00 P.M. train into Essex on Friday, February 16, arrived at 11.00 P.M., and the *Gloucester Times* reported that the past few days had seen the worst weather of the winter. Amid all this, Mrs. Louis Burnham was operated on for appendicitis in her home on Martin Street, Dr. Johnson of Beverly performing the surgery. Moreover, there seemed to be little slackening in social affairs. At the weekly meeting of the Knights of Pythias the brothers voted to buy and install a radio for the entertainment of the members and their friends at the lodge hall over Quint's drug store. The T.N.T. (Thimble, Needle and Thread) Club of the Universalist Church, as they had for years, served a fine chicken pie supper on Washington's Birthday, followed this time by a one-act comedy "The Rag Carpet Bee." Up at the high school a group from neighboring Hamilton challenged the local team to a debate on the subject "Resolved: that movies do more harm than good."

With the completion of planking, *Columbia* did indeed become a real ship and, with no slackening of pace, work began on the installation of the heavy deck framework. While this was going on, caulkers Len Amero, Bill Atkins and George Story went about their work of filling the seams of the hull first with a strand or "thread" of cotton and then with two threads of oakum. Behind came our friend Sammy Gray to putty and trowel off the tops of the seams, and following Sammy came the outboard joiners, John "Skeet" Doyle and Alan Brewton. Their job was to smooth and plane with their wooden hand planes the whole exterior of the hull. Down at the after end of the ship, Tom Irving began his task of making *Columbia's* big rudder, the rudder which was to play such a crucial part in subsequent events of *Columbia's* career.

Putting in the great beams which formed the deck structure was no operation for lightweights, either. Beams were of white oak and generally "sided" eight inches (horizontal dimension). Their molded (vertical) dimension would vary from perhaps six inches at the sides of the vessel to as much as nine inches at the center. Through the middle of the ship they were twenty-five feet long and each, of course, was crowned or curved upward to allow the

74

deck to shed water. Each was meticulously cut to lock into the supporting shelf structure at the sides, and framework for all deck openings was carefully mortised in. Underneath, in the way of the masts, were fitted the large hackmatack knees imported from Canada.

They finished *Columbia's* deck framing on Saturday, the third of March. That same day the *Mayflower* was hauled on the Parkhurst railways at Gloucester. With the economic facts of life staring them in the face, her owners had at length concluded that the time had come to put an engine in and work was about to begin. While at Gloucester she was also to have her beautiful spars cut down to a more practical working size. Any further thought that *Mayflower* might again contend for the Dennis Trophy was gone with the wind. For anyone who cared to see it, the lesson was there that a vessel built and rigged to be a racer was not much by way of a money maker.

In Essex it was town meeting time; the first Monday in March had been town meeting day for generations. Proceedings were relatively mild compared to some years. As a result of stirring speeches by Frank McKenzie and Ezra Hinckley, it was voted to spend $1,000 to institute an organized police force for the town. The man chosen to be chief of the new force was Essex River pilot Thales Cook at a salary of $500 per year, he to furnish his own uniform and transportation (except for court attendance). His patrol duty would be from 2 to 8 p.m. each day from May to October, although he was to be on call at all times. The meeting further decided to retain the "moonlight" plan for the operation of street lights. Under this scheme it was customary to extinguish the streetlights on nights of bright moonlight as an economy measure. Of course, the street lights were always turned off at 1:00 A.M. anyway.

On Wednesday, March 7, the worst blizzard of the whole winter hit Essex and Cape Ann. Again the trains were hours late and the Fordson tractor hired from the Gloucester Autobus Co. to clear the main streets was taxed to capacity. It was the first winter it had been used and the citizens in town meeting had felt the $200 it cost was well worth it. That Friday the P.T.A. sponsored a public speaking contest and athletic exhibition with Indian clubs and dumbbells at the town hall. The affair was a huge success. Somehow in spite of its reluctance to leave, people realized that winter was on the wane and took heart from the appearing signs of spring.

Columbia, too, was showing signs that it would not be long before launching time. By Saint Patrick's day her rail stanchions were in and the bulwarks well along; her white pine deck was laid and caulking started and the great snow banks which had enveloped the ship were fast receding. At the other end of the yard, her companion of the winter, the *Marjorie Parker,* was primed and had her name boards on.

With the completion of the deck, it was possible for work below to get under way. The building of the forecastle was in the capable hands of Jack Doyle, a man of long experience. It was his job first to help install the big cypress water tanks and then to build the forecastle floor over them. With that finished, he built berths, lockers, ice chest, coal bin, gangway, galley and table for a complement of eighteen men. Jack, too, was a loner and had a tremendous capacity for work, doing alone what in other yards was handled by at least two men.

While Jack handled the forecastle, Ed Perkins was building the cabin trunk and the after cabin. Ed was of a long line of Yankee ship-joiners and was an artisan of the highest order. Through long years of craftsmanship he had always observed the old maxim that "a job worth doing at all is worth doing well." It was Ed who once advised a fellow workman to "do the best you can and when you get it done it won't be any better than it ought to be." In his hands the main cabin trunk on the raised deck aft took shape together with skylight and companionway. Below, he had built the quarters for the captain and five more of the crew.

There was much to be done on deck with hatch coamings and companionways to build, rail cap to be put on, bitts and chocks to be put in, and chain plates and iron work for the rigging to be installed. These were being capably handled by Arthur Norton, Tom Irving, Jack Murphy and Leandre Doucette. Cut-

76

ting the many holes for masts, portlights, pumps and hawse pipes was Stanwood Burnham, better known to all as Needles. Needles derived his appellation from the fact that whether he needed it or not, he shaved regularly—every Saturday. Further, it had been his habit as a younger man to wear shoes with long needle-like toes. He once sat in on a poker game and before starting to play asked one of the boys if he could borrow two dollars. "All I've got is a five," was the reply. "That's all right. I can change it," said Needles. He took his civic responsibilities very seriously, serving the town as moth superintendent and always making a point to attend town meetings. Since he had no family and owned no real estate, he felt that as merely a payer of poll tax he had no moral right to vote on fiscal matters and scrupulously refrained from doing so.

They put the bowsprit in on Tuesday, March 27. At that point launching day was to be three weeks away. If *Columbia* was to meet the stipulation of the Deed of Gift and be off to sea by April 30, there was no time to lose. All of the thousand odd jobs and loose ends must still be completed and those oft-styled "finishing touches" would have to hurry. But A. D. Story was never one to get much excited about anything. He and the gang reasoned that it was nobody's fault the winter had been one of the worst on record; every man was doing the best he could and one couldn't ask more than that. Except for the weather, *Columbia* would have been ready to go before now. In the relatively mild winter of 1921 we recall that *Mayflower* had been finished in fifty-nine working days, albeit it took a double gang concentrating on the one job to do it.

Sunday, April 1, was Easter. The temperature that morning was 8 degrees, with snowbanks still in evidence. As on every Sunday morning, A. D. Story was in pew 65 of the Congregational Church. To his mind the tenets of an old New England Protestant faith and the welfare of his church were quite as important as anything that could be taking place in his shipyard. He was then and had been for years a member of the governing parish committee and had participated in the life of the church since boyhood. That Sunday was to be the last one for the old pipe organ. On her own responsibility, Mrs. Florence Goodhue, the organist, had gone out and raised the money for a new one, the installation of which was to start directly. Evidently the ceiling in the sanctuary got wind of this and decided that if the organ was going, it was going too. It fell down that week. Luckily it waited, but that only made another problem for the parish committee. It wasn't enough that they'd been trying all winter to find a new minister.

It was also an eventful week in both shipyards. At James' they launched the *Isabel Q.* They had a little birthday party there, too, as caulker Luther E. Burnham celebrated his seventy-fourth birthday by passing out cigars to all hands. On Saturday it was time to launch the *Marjorie Parker.* A large crowd of spectators was on hand to see her take the plunge, and their autos lined Main Street on both sides and across the causeway joining Essex and South Essex. Adding to the marine traffic were the tug *Eveleth,* come to get the *Parker,* the *Isabel Q.* and the workboats and tug of the dredging company whose labors had now resumed.

With the *Marjorie Parker* out of the way, the Story gang could devote its full attention to getting *Columbia* ready. Even though he had a few odds and ends still to finish up in the forecastle, A. D. brought Jack Doyle out to lead the building of the launchways. (This was another of his specialties.) With an important vessel of such size and depth and with a crowd expected, an upright launching in a proper cradle was to be used rather than the gung-ho side or bilge launching commonly used in Essex for the run-of-the-mill fishermen. Aboard, others of the men were cleaning chips and shavings out of the bilges; Ed Perkins was hurrying to finish the cabin; George Story and the caulkers were trying to finish up the after deck, and the final coat of paint was being applied to the outside of the hull. In her color scheme *Columbia* represented something of a departure from custom in that Ben Pine wanted a medium gray for the topsides with white bulwarks. It gave her a sleeker, more "yachty" appearance. Usually a fisherman was painted gloss black clear to the tops of the rail caps.

78

It was tentatively expected that *Columbia* would be ready by Saturday, April 14. However, it appeared, as the week wore on, that Monday or Tuesday of the following week would be more like it. A. D. was not overly fond of having a large crowd underfoot on launching day and so purposely kept the final progress rather quiet. It was bad enough that reporters and groups of the curious were already nosing about and getting in the way. A bad case of "race fever" was slowly building up again in the region, and the Boston papers had not allowed the finishing of *Columbia* to go unnoticed. By Saturday of that week A. D. and the Columbia Associates decided that the following Tuesday, April 17, would be the day.

That night a fine bean supper was served in the basement of the Methodist Church. As he often did on such occasions, Nathan Holmes slid the beans he couldn't eat into his coat pocket for use at a later date. For entertainment following the supper "Shine" Wilson put on a demonstration of paper tearing and, with George Story, rendered a few rousing harmonica duets. On Monday night the annual meeting of the Congregational parish elected B. F. Raymond, Caleb Low and A. D. Story to be members of the parish committee for the ensuing year. Frank E. Burnham was elected clerk.

Early next morning, the roaring of a plumber's furnace was heard in the Story shipyard as Jack Doyle and his crew melted the paraffin candles to cover the ground ways. The paraffin would make a base coat for the ways, to which the thick yellow launching grease would stick. Elsewhere the gang was taking down what little was left of the staging and removing the heavy shores which had supported *Columbia* all these weeks. The launching cradle would support her until she became waterborne. A bundle of six heavy timbers was rigged to check the vessel's momentum. A. D. often planned to have a launching vessel drag the keel pieces of the next vessel into place. In this case the drag was made up of the keel timbers for the schooner *Shamrock*, yet another racing contender soon to take shape in the berth about to be vacated by *Columbia*.

There was no desire for a repetition of last year's fiasco when

Henry Ford became stuck fast in the mud, so it was planned that *Columbia* hit the water with the tide still coming. As soon as word came that the tug was in the river, the men began to split away the blocks. By this process the weight of the ship was transferred from the blocks and cribbing on which she had been built to the cradle in which she would slide into the water. With that done, all was in readiness for the great moment. In spite of attempts to keep it quiet, a goodly delegation of master mariners from Gloucester were on hand and a sizable crowd had gathered. To minimize any danger involved, the man who was to skipper the vessel, Capt. Alden Geele, and the sponsor, Miss Gertrude Cary of Lawrence, climbed to the deck, where Miss Cary smashed a bottle of "real champagne" over the port bow. Then they climbed back down, the deck was cleared of everyone and the men took up the crosscut saws. It was 11:40 A.M. As they had done for the *Henry Ford*, it was Jake Story and Sammy Gray manning the saw on the port ways and Willard Andrews and John Murphy on the starboard ways. At the word from Jack Doyle they sawed down to the first mark, then, pausing to synchronize their strokes, they sawed for dear life and *Columbia* was on her way.

Majestically she gained momentum, her big name banner and the American flag stretched to the breeze. Reaching the way ends and with a rending and cracking of her cradle, she made a splendid plunge into the Essex River. As she glided to the end of her tether she was greeted with a blast from the whistle of the big Boston tug *Confidence*, come to get her, and the horns of the autos parked about the river basin. Here were sights and sounds to quicken anyone's pulse. It was a perfect launching—almost. Somehow A. D. had neglected to put the usual timber braces on the rudder to hold it straight and fast during entry into the water. Instead the wheel had been lashed from on deck. It was noticed by some that the rudder had twisted around to starboard as she hit the water. However, when the men went aboard, the lashings were still there and all seemed in order as they made ready to be taken in tow. As far as anyone could tell, she

Columbia. Kupsinel photo courtesy Charles F. Sayle

Finishing the framing with the hanging of the forward cants. International News photo

Columbia is framed out, the rabbet has been cut and planking begins. John Hubbard here prepares to start dubbing for the garboard streak (the string over his head is for fairing). International News photo

March 17, 1923: *Columbia* is planked, the first pieces of waist are on and the deck largely complete. Photo E. J. Story

The day before launching. Contrary to the Gloucester practice of having a schooner's topsides black, Ben Pine had the *Columbia*'s bulwarks painted white, the wales light gray. The vertical line is from a crack in the glass-plate negative. Photo E. J. Story in the Peabody Museum, Salem

Tuesday, April 17, 1923: *Columbia* glides into the Essex River as the supporting cradle breaks away. The usual timber braces for the rudder are not used. Photo E. J. Story

The Confidence with *Columbia* in tow starts down the Essex River toward Gloucester, where spars, rigging and outfit will be put aboard. Photo E. J. Story

The "antagonists" Angus Walters (left) and Ben Pine on the deck of *Columbia*. Photo Charles F. Sayle

Workmen busily prepare *Columbia* before her sailing from Gloucester. Under racing rules a new vessel must have left her last port of call by April 30. Photo Peabody Museum, Salem

On deck during one of *Columbia*'s trial spins in preparation for racing.
Photo Peabody Museum, Salem

Columbia as she lay for most of 1925 by the salt wharf in East Gloucester. Photo Charles F. Sayle

Captain Mat Critchett (foot on hatch coaming) talks with Ben Pine as the lumpers discharge a cargo of Newfoundland herring in February 1927. Standing by is Deputy Collector of Customs O'Brien, Gloucester. Photo Peabody Museum, Salem

Putting the rails under on a port tack. It slows the vessel but is great sport for the fishermen. Photo Charles F. Sayle

Columbia following close on the *Henry Ford* in 1926. Kupsinel photo courtesy Gloucester Camera and Photo Shop

responded to her helm as she should, and so, with a hawser from the *Confidence*, she started the trip to Gloucester. Gliding slowly around the bends of the river she displayed her beauty of sheer and form to the onlookers on shore. Many remarked that here was one of the most beautiful schooners yet to come from the yards at Essex.

To knowledgeable observers, *Columbia* seemed to be a very graceful craft with a particularly beautiful profile, both above and below the water. Her bilges were very high and slack, giving the impression, especially before painting, that she had no bilges at all. Final painting, of course, changed her appearance greatly, and the removal of all staging before launching brought the true shape of the hull clearly into view. Her rail line seemed more peaked and narrowed in both fore and aft than the *Puritan*; where *Puritan*'s bow sections had been something of a V-shape, *Columbia*'s were more rounded. *Columbia* seemed to have a degree of tumble-home for most of the length of her rail. Aft and below the water, the rabbet line rose up across the deadwood, leaving much of the dead wood exposed, and her mid-ship section was less of an S-curve than *Puritan*'s had been. Some who looked at her believed that had Starling Burgess retained some of the broad flat stern which characterized *Mayflower*, the new vessel might have more stability in a strong wind.

Thus was *Columbia* born. Starting on December 4, 1922, she had been built in 115 working days by a shipyard force which, over that period, had numbered exactly thirty men. Of these only fourteen men were there for the whole period. Others had come and gone or had been there for varying periods. One man had lasted only six days and another only eleven. Of those 115 days, thirty were stormy or days of severe weather, including a total of thirteen when it was too bad for any work at all. Thus it can be said that *Columbia* was actually built in 102 working days. During the same period another smaller schooner had been nearly all built and a third vessel was started and partly framed out. Although the *Columbia* was designed by Starling Burgess,

Ben Pine and A.D. Story together had made certain minor modifications in the bow and stern. Ben also was later to incorporate a number of his own ideas into the rigging.

The *Confidence*, with *Columbia* in tow and Essex pilot (now chief of police) Thales Cook to guide her, steamed out of Essex River and around Cape Ann, arriving in Gloucester about 2:30 P.M., where she was docked beneath the shears at Burnham's railways. Immediately, rigger George Roberts, himself one of the Columbia Associates, and his men started their work, and in the record time of three and one-half hours had the spars all stepped. Usually it took nearly six hours to do this job.

The handling of the spars was itself an interesting procedure. They had been made by George E. Thurston at his shop on Gloucester's Commercial Street. The mainmast was a little less than ninety-five feet long and the foremast about eighty-five feet. The spar shop backed up to the harbor, and the masts, when finished, were slid overboard and floated to the wharf where they were to be installed. The foremast was hoisted from the water first. With each they paused with the mast resting across the vessel's rails and the mast-head on the wharf while the crosstrees were slid into place.

With spars in, *Columbia* was taken next morning to Ben Pine's Atlantic Supply Co. wharf and the work of rigging and outfitting began in earnest. A gang of A. D. Story's carpenters were there to complete their work, a couple of caulkers were endeavoring to finish up the after deck, the riggers were clambering all over the ship and painters were doing what they had to do. Amidst all were the frenetic traffickings of unidentified artisans and crowds of the curious come to inspect seemingly every nook and cranny of the ship. The whole presented a picture of utter chaos. Nevertheless, in spite of it all, rigger Roberts was able to set the standing rigging that forenoon and give it its first stretching.

Uppermost in every mind was that crucial date, April 30. If *Columbia* was to meet it, she must be away from Gloucester in one week and there was so much to do. Still, another of Captain Geele's boats, the big *Tattler*, had been exactly one week from launching to maiden trip, so it wasn't impossible. Though normally a Massachusetts holiday, April 19 afforded no respite to the workmen aboard *Columbia*. The riggers got the main topmast up while other workers were stowing ballast. For the first trip at least she would sail without a fore topmast. On Friday they gave the standing rigging its second pull. It was noted with some interest in Gloucester that another Canadian contender had been launched the day before from the yard of John MacLean & Sons in Mahone Bay, N.S. Called the *Kene*, she was designed by C. A. MacLean for Capt. Albert Himmelman. Her dimensions were very close to those of *Bluenose*.

On Monday morning a rather heavy rain prevented the riggers from working outside, but the carpenters carried on their work in the fish hold and the ironworkers finished up their work on the windlass. By afternoon it let up and the booms and gaffs, newly arrived from Thurston's spar shop, were hung, allowing the riggers to set the running rigging and start bending on sail. Early Tuesday morning found *Columbia* towed to the salt wharf, where she shipped 450 hogsheads of salt, immediately returning to the Atlantic Supply wharf to resume taking on stores. With luck they hoped she would be ready to sail next day. Some idea of what was involved can be gained by a perusal of the following list of stores and supplies put aboard *Columbia* for her maiden fishing trip, these to last a crew of twenty-four from three to four months:

600 lbs. of tobacco, plus that which crew would bring aboard	24 bottles vanilla extract
	25 lbs. prunes
	48 pkgs. pudding
16 barrels of flour	24 bottles ketchup
1100 lbs. of sugar	12 mugs prepared mustard
60 lbs. of tea	25 pkgs. currants
40 lbs. of coffee	15 lbs. barley
7 bushels of beans	25 lbs. evaporated peaches
1 bushel of dry beans	100 lbs. fresh meat
60 bushels of potatoes	24 lbs. cheese
5 bushels of turnips	100 lbs. slack salted pollock
1 barrel of corned shoulder	40 bars soap
1 barrel of salt pork	25 pkgs. washing powder

300 lbs. salt spare ribs
200 lbs. smoked ham
11 barrels of beef
75 lbs. of raisins
100 cans of evaporated apples
120 gals. of kerosene
16 cases of milk
15 gals. molasses
50 lbs. rice
150 lbs. onions
4 cases eggs
300 cans of beets, squash, string beans, blueberries, corn, peas, peaches, tomatoes and clams
40 lbs. crackers
40 lbs. baking powder
15 cans cream of tartar
15 lbs. salaratus
2 to 4 lbs. each of nutmeg, pepper, allspice, clove, ginger, cassia and mustard
20 pkgs. cornstarch
30 boxes salt
60 lbs. jam
30 lbs. lemon pie filling
20 lbs. mincemeat
24 bottles lemon extract

24 pkgs. soap powder
24 gross of matches
6 tons coal
4 bundles kindling
450 hogsheads of salt
3 gross wax candles
20 yds. towelling
25 yds. torch wicking
1 doz. torches
4 coils buoy line
30 doz. 7 lb. lines
10 doz. 22 lb. lines
700 lbs. of lead (for sinkers)
24 dory gaffs
18 fish forks
20 pairs of oars
32 10 lb. anchors
30 gal. gasoline
36 prs. of rubber boots
20 doz. pairs of cotton gloves
5 doz. pairs of cotton mitts
150 yds. of cotton cloth for dory sails
4 doz. suits of oil skins
1 doz. oiled petticoats
24 bail buckets
28 mattresses
24 water jugs

Also, there were dishes, crockery, silverware, cooking utensils, tools, dory tackle, painters, and so forth, plus twenty-four single dories taken on in Nova Scotia. One wonders how with all that stuff aboard there would be room for a crew of twenty-four to rest their weary bones, let alone find a place to stow any fish.

Although a mighty effort was made to wind things up for a Wednesday sailing, it was just not possible. Furthermore, Captain Geele was feeling a little "off the hooks" that afternoon, which, added to the fact that a head wind from the northeast was blowing, led him to decide to wait for the morrow. When Thursday morning came, it again brought with it a gang of riggers, shipsmiths, iron workers and some of Story's carpenters in a desperate attempt to finish. All were taken for an impromptu ride when at 10:30 the tug came and took the ship on a turn about the harbor to adjust her compass. Back at the wharf the preparations were at long last complete or at least as complete as they were going to be. Captain Geele paced the wharf, puffing on his pipe and eager to be away. He was besieged by a battery of photographers. In the expectation that *Columbia* might not leave with time enough to meet the letter of the Deed of Gift, Ben and the Gloucester race committee had wired the Trustees at Halifax requesting a few days of grace. It was explained that any delay was occasioned by the unusual severity of the past winter which had slowed the progress of the work. Happily, the Trustees granted "a reasonable time" to complete outfitting and start the first cruise. One of their own boats had been so hindered.

Early that afternoon came the culmination of all the months of struggle as Captain Geele cast off the lines and *Columbia* sailed on her maiden trip. As she headed out past Dogbar breakwater she was escorted by a number of small craft, while groups of people gathered at vantage points along the shore to see her go. Clearing the harbor she shaped a course to the east'rd, bound out on a dory handlining trip. The Columbia Associates expressed themselves as being well pleased and more than satisfied with their new schooner, which had cost a little less than $35,000 exclusive of outfit.

Capt. Alden Geele, *Columbia's* first commander, was a tall, spare rather serious man of fifty-nine. Born in Waldoboro, Maine, he first fished as a young man out of Portland, but after a couple of years came to Gloucester, where he remained. For many seasons he had been the skipper of the *Tattler*, the largest two-masted vessel out of Gloucester, and while in the *Tattler* he made the largest catches of salt fish ever recorded in that port. On the 6th of September, 1916, he arrived in Gloucester with a trip of 500,000 lbs. of salt cod which sold for $21,000. It proved to be the largest trip ever made in the dory handline fishery.

Although potentially a very beautiful ship, *Columbia* was certainly not much to look at as she left Gloucester harbor for the

85

first time. As yet she had no mainsail and with no mainsail or main gaff she could not, of course, carry a main topsail. She also had no fore topmast and therefore could carry no fore topsail. As she left she carried her regular jib, jumbo and foresail plus the curious three-cornered riding sail rigged in place of her main. Aloft there was a rather ill-fitting main topmast (or fisherman's) staysail. With this truncated rig she was to fish throughout her first trip. She certainly made a rather forlorn comparison to the maiden departures of her sisters of the year before, sailing as they did under full press of canvas amid such loud acclaim.

In spite of the fact that *Columbia* was leaving Gloucester on April 26, this did not count under the rules, for she was still not ready to commence fishing. She must first go to Shelburne, N.S., for yet a few more stores and for her dories. In those days American vessels bought many dories at Shelburne, where they could be had for twenty-five dollars apiece. More importantly, it would be in Shelburne that Capt. Geele would have to fill out his crew, since in the later years of salt fishing Gloucester boats were dependent upon Nova Scotia for crewmen.

Columbia arrived in Shelburne on April 28, just fifty-two hours out of Gloucester. This wasn't too bad considering that she carried no mainsail. Light airs across the bay gave little opportunity to try her speed, but a nasty chop left over from the departing northeaster showed her to be easy in a seaway. Ben Pine and a couple of newspapermen had come along for the ride and to lend Captain Geele a hand. During the night of her arrival *Columbia*, riding at the end of thirty fathoms of cable, pulled her 800 pound anchor out of the mud and started up the harbor. Captain Geele, Ben Pine and the newspapermen, all sleeping aboard, tumbled on deck to bend on the other 800 pound hook. Somehow they managed to wrestle it over the rail and *Columbia* fetched up barely 100 yards from the nasty ledge under her stern. She had dragged over a quarter of a mile. Captain Geele, who had been going in and out of Shelburne for thirty years, declared it to be the first time he had ever heard of a vessel being blown off an anchorage in that harbor.

While in Shelburne, Ben and Captain Geele received the notice from Mr. Dennis and Mr. Silver, chairman of the Trustees, that "all reasonable allowances would be made for delays over which the owners and captain had no control." Since many of the men who planned to come to Shelburne to join the *Columbia* were coming by water, the windy weather delayed them for still a few more days, and it was not until May 8 that *Columbia* really began her work-a-day career.

5 ★ The First Summer

On a so-called dory handlining trip, the vessel, after arriving on the fishing grounds, put out her dories with one man in each. The fishermen rowed to a likely spot and put over two lines, each with a lead sinker and two hooks on it. Salted clams were a commonly used bait and the catch was generally cod. The dory loads of cod were brought back to the vessel where they were cleaned, split and gutted and stowed below in layers of rock salt, one barrel of salt being required for every barrel of fish.

The common handlining single (one man) dories such as *Columbia* carried were thirteen feet long, measured along their bottoms. *Columbia* carried twenty-four of these dories. A thirteen-foot dory could carry up to 1,700 pounds of fish. Fully equipped for fishing, each carried the following equipment: one pair of eight-foot ash oars; one or two pairs of cotton or woolen mitts (gloves with no fingers, also called "nippers"); two hand lines, fifty fathoms each, on reels, with a three and a half pound lead and two hooks attached; bait bucket; bait board; lunch box; spare hooks; a gaff; bait knife; water jug and a "gob-stick." Sometimes they carried a dory compass and each, of course, had an anchor and anchor rode. The dory itself had a painter, stern becket, thole pins, thwart and two "kid boards" designed to keep the fish from sliding into the spot where the fisherman was working. A "gob stick" (generally a sawed-off piece of an old handle) was used to run down the throat of a fish to disengage a swallowed hook.

The fisherman worked standing in his dory with a cod line in each hand, moving them up and down with the baited hooks just clear of the bottom. Both lines were made fast to the dory. When he got a bite, he dropped one line and pulled in the other, using the dory gaff to flip the larger fish into the boat. Quickly unhooking, he would re-bait and heave the line clear of the dory. When fish were biting fast he was a very busy man. It took a good deal of expertise, too, for a man to stand up and keep his balance while fishing from a rolling and pitching little dory.

The lack of a mainsail on *Columbia* was not as important as it might at first seem, since the mainsail was taken in anyway when a vessel arrived on the fishing grounds. A riding sail such as *Columbia* set was hoisted in its place and served to steady the ship against excessive rolling and to keep her head to the wind. Forward they usually set foresail and jumbo. "Ready to go housekeeping" was the expression the fishermen used when a vessel had anchored on the grounds and was ready to put out the dories. These would be put over at the start of each day, with the men rowing off in all directions to start their fishing. A fishing trip of this kind lasted until a vessel was full, generally a period of from two to three months. During that time, if a schooner was using fresh bait, she occasionally put in at a Nova Scotia or Newfoundland port for more bait or a few supplies, but often they were out there for the whole period.

Columbia did very well on her first trip, arriving back in Gloucester on Wednesday, June 27, having been gone exactly two months. She hailed for 324,000 pounds of salt cod, most of which had been caught on Sable Island Bank. Her maiden stock was $12,693 with a share of $261 for each of the crew. She had met with very severe weather on several occasions and Captain Geele said that in all his thirty years on the water he had never set foot on the deck of a finer craft than *Columbia*. He was not, however, able to test fully her sailing qualities in the absence of a proper mainsail. This was to be remedied as Ben Pine borrowed a mainsail from the *Elizabeth Howard*, a vessel which he managed, and when *Columbia* sailed again on Thursday, July 5, she had her fore topmast in and a full suit of canvas. Once more she was bound on a dory handlining trip.

The year was 1923, which, as we mentioned at the beginning of this narrative, was the year in which Gloucester was to celebrate the 300th anniversary of the coming of the first white settlers. An elaborate observance was planned. There would, of course, be a number of affairs for the tea-cup set, but as far as the waterfront was concerned, the only event worth mentioning was the planned "Anniversary Race." The committee in charge was going all out to make it a bang-up contest. There would be *Columbia*, Ben Pine's *Elizabeth Howard*, and if Clayt Morrissey could be talked into it, the *Henry Ford*. It was rumored that *Mayflower* would take off her propeller and come down for a try, and, as a gesture of international good will, an invitation was sent to all fishing schooners of Nova Scotia and Newfoundland. The O'Hara Brothers of Boston entered the name of their new schooner *Shamrock* although she was still on the ways at Story's in Essex. The winner of the race was to be awarded the Lipton Cup, put up by the doughty Sir Thomas Lipton some years earlier and last won by the *Rose Dorothea* in 1907.

Plans were well under way when word reached Gloucester that *Columbia* had been in collision with the big French steam trawler *La Champlain* off the northeast bar of Sable Island. The report went on to say that she had been hit on the port side and that her forward rigging and bowsprit were carried away and considerable damage done to the forward rail. It said the damage was confined to an area above the waterline and the trawler had towed *Columbia* into St. Pierre for temporary repairs. Gloucester heaved a collective sigh of relief, although disappointed that she would not be home for Monday, August 27.

As hoped, the *Henry Ford* arrived home from her second trip of the season on Monday, August 13, hailing for 240,000 pounds of salt fish. At noon the next day, old trooper that he was, Captain Morrissey went up the street and registered for the race with the official at the Gloucester National Bank. Saturday of that week was the occasion of another big affair in Essex as the time had come for Story to launch the new *Shamrock*, entered as a race contestant some three weeks before. With another vessel being completed in the yard and A. D. laid up a couple of weeks with water on the knee, she hadn't come along quite as fast as had been expected, although in the last weeks they had really hustled to have her ready on time.

In the prevailing atmosphere of racing excitement, a crowd estimated to be bigger than the one that had gathered for *May-*

90

flower jammed the area around the shipyard, and in places the narrow Essex streets were three-deep in parked cars. It was a fine day and the launching went off perfectly, the crowd roaring its approval much to the satisfaction of A. D. and the gang. Again the *Confidence* was there, and taking *Shamrock* in tow, quickly arrived at Gloucester, where there would be exactly one week to get the new vessel rigged and ready to sail.

The big celebration got under way on Saturday, August 25. Civic events of all kinds were scheduled for each day of the following week. Extra cars were added to all incoming trains, and special trains were scheduled to return to Boston each evening. As race time drew near there had been no response from Canada, and *Mayflower's* owners sent word that she was still fishing, therefore leaving *Henry Ford, Elizabeth Howard* and *Shamrock* as the only entries. The race was scheduled for Monday, but when Monday came, a combination of fog and no wind forced a postponement till Thursday so as not to conflict with other scheduled events. However, disappointment at this was greatly tempered with the arrival in the city that morning of none other than the jovial Sir Thomas Lipton himself, come to greet the competing skippers. The 5th Infantry Band met Sir Thomas at Blynman bridge and escorted him and his companion, Mayor John F. Fitzgerald of Boston, to Post Office Square in the heart of Gloucester, where they were greeted by Gloucester Mayor William J. MacInnis and a tremendous throng. They next visited the *Shamrock* down at the Gas Light wharf and afterwards, in the company of Captain Morrissey, Captain Pine and Capt. Marty Welch, picked to be skipper of *Shamrock*, they all posed with the Lipton Trophy in front of the Gloucester National Bank.

On Thursday morning the *Shamrock, Elizabeth Howard* and *Henry Ford* appeared at the starting line, the *Henry Ford* proudly sporting a brand new mainsail presented by the friends of Captain Morrissey and cut the way he wanted it. Again there were very light airs and the start was delayed an hour and a half to 10:30, at which time, with the promise of a rising breeze, the schooners were off.

91

First over the mark was Marty Welch and his *Shamrock* with *Ford* 50 seconds behind. As they approached the first mark the *Ford* overhauled *Shamrock*, and rounding the buoy it was *Ford*, *Shamrock* and *Howard*. At this point Marty Welch and Ben Pine in the *Howard* engaged in a fierce luffing match, enabling Clayt Morrissey and the *Ford* to go far in the lead. The wind, however, died and at the expiration of the six-hour time limit the leading *Henry Ford* was still miles from the finish, so it had to be declared "no race."

They started again the next day after a second postponement in the hope of more wind. This time the *Howard* was first over the line with *Henry Ford* second, although with such headway she immediately shot into the lead. It was a good race to the first mark, where the *Ford* led the *Howard* by 35 seconds and *Shamrock* 20 seconds behind that. The next leg was a seven and one-half mile beat to windward and it was *Henry Ford* all the way, but Captain Morrissey overstood the mark and, by the time he rounded, had only a two and one-half minute lead over the *Howard*. *Shamrock* was eight minutes behind *Howard*.

The next two legs were slacked sheets for another fifteen miles with a freshening breeze. The schooners tore along with Ben Pine beginning to overtake the *Henry Ford* and picking up over a minute and a half. On the last leg, a close fetch for the finish line five miles away. Ben did his best, picking up another 11 seconds, but Captain Clayt in the *Henry Ford* held his lead and at the line was 50 seconds ahead of *Elizabeth Howard*, winning the race, the Lipton Trophy and a purse of $1,000. Second place *Elizabeth Howard* won the John W. Prentiss Cup and a purse of $800. Last place *Shamrock* won $800 but no cup. It all had been a most satisfying affair.

It is interesting to take note of the situation here in the case of *Shamrock*. Yachtsmen and sailing people were no doubt struck with the fact of a brand new wooden vessel not twelve days off the builder's ways taking part in a race. She had barely managed to be rigged, let alone have a chance to do any tuning up, yet a man like Marty Welch could take her and make a very creditable showing in spite of this and in spite of the fact also that she was smaller than her two competitors.

On Friday, the 14th of September, *Columbia* arrived home, her second trip shortened somewhat first by the collision and then by a shortage of bait. This time she hailed for a mere 225,000 pounds of salt cod, stocking $9,011 with a share of $166. As to the collision, it appeared she had been more sideswiped than rammed. She had been struck while at anchor and her forward rigging on the port side had been torn away, with the rail split for many feet. Seams were opened up, some badly, from the stem clear back to the main rigging. The stem itself was sprung slightly to starboard and the bowsprit was carried away, splitting the heel of the sampson post as it went.

It appeared at the time of the accident as if the vessel would go to the bottom, and all hands abandoned ship; however, it shortly became apparent that *Columbia* was not going to sink immediately and Captain Geele ordered the crew to return and try to save her. Believing their ship to be doomed, the crew refused the order. For one of the two times in his long career as a master, Captain Geele was forced to threaten the men with his pistol. He assured them he would use it unless they returned and manned the pumps. In the face of this threat the men reboarded the vessel and were able to lower the water and keep ahead of it while the trawler which had struck them towed *Columbia* to St. Pierre.

Coincidentally with *Columbia*'s arrival back in Gloucester, the *Bluenose* arrived home in Lunenburg with a good trip of 2,700 quintals of codfish. She was welcomed by a salvo from a cannon on the wharf. To date she had brought in the largest catch of any vessel in the Lunenburg fleet that season.

The following Monday *Columbia*'s fare was sold to the Fred L. Davis Co. and even as the lumpers began to discharge the cargo the riggers began to repair the damaged shrouds. As soon as the cargo was out it was planned to haul the vessel on the railways to commence the hull repairs so that *Columbia* would be in good shape for the elimination race scheduled for October 12.

Now that the season's international competition was close at hand, the American Race Committee began to study the new fine print in the Deed of Gift. Doing so led them to believe that not one of the available American contenders would be eligible for competition. The root of the matter lay in the basic difference between Canadian and American schooners. While generally very similar, the Canadian schooners had a tendency to be somewhat higher sided and with a rather squatty rig. This reflected a common practice of using their vessels for salt banking in the summer and for freighting in the winter months. American vessels, on the other hand, showed a preference for low freeboard and a loftier rig, making for easier dory handling and enabling them to make fast runs to market if fresh fish was aboard, both summer and winter. With sections of the rules dealing now in matters of spar lengths and freeboard it began to look to the American committee as though the Canadians were trying to protect their *Bluenose* and to apply a Canadian yardstick to the construction of American vessels.

The latest controversy began in early September when a request was received in Gloucester from the Trustees that a set of plans of each possible American contender be sent to Halifax for examination to determine the vessel's compliance with regulations. The Americans replied by stating they wanted a "vessel for vessel" race with no restrictions and that any American entry should be accepted "as is." To clarify matters, a sub-committee was delegated to go to Nova Scotia and confer with the Canadians; however, it was found to be impossible to arrange a time of meeting that would be mutually acceptable. Failing this, they resorted to a voluminous exchange of telegrams. At length the American committee, feeling they were getting nowhere, sent word that if the present rules were to be strictly observed, the whole business would be called off and the Gloucester vessels would stay home. To this the Trustees sent a wire requesting that only the dimensions of *Columbia* be sent. This was done, and on the 4th of October word was received from the Trustees that *Columbia* would be eligible to race. To quote their telegram: "Measurements given for *Columbia* made her eligible as chal-

94

lenger under this year's rules except slight difference in freeboard which Trustees are willing to concede. If any other previously constructed vessel is nominated, she must comply with last year's rules regarding draft, water line, sail area, etc. October 20 suggested as date first race."

It appears that the bone of contention here centered on the fact that *Columbia*'s freeboard did not in fact comply with the letter of the new measurement regulations and was also less than that of *Bluenose*. In sending the requested information to the Trustees, Captain Pine expressed the opinion of Columbia Associates that such a request was not warranted by any condition of the Deed of Gift or rules of procedure adopted thereunder. However, they "felt that a frank compliance with the request could not but lend itself to a better feeling and understanding." They further stated that the measurement in question on *Columbia* was "within five inches of that specified in the Deed of Gift and it seems inconceivable that a point of such small importance could be used by anyone to disqualify a vessel which has proved herself in every way an unusually able, comfortable and efficient craft for the purpose of going after and staying until she gets a full fare of fish, whether fresh or salt."

The "previously constructed vessel" mentioned in the reply of the Trustees was an obvious reference to *Henry Ford*, and in this connection the American committee was emphatic in their feeling that if an elimination race could be held in time, and if it were won by the *Ford*, the Canadians would have to accept her "as is." Captain Morrissey had been most outspoken in his statements that under no circumstances would he tolerate any sail-cutting "monkeyshines" again this year, race or no race.

All of this lengthy and rather acrimonious exchange had extended throughout the whole month of September and into October with a resulting uncertainty as to any possibility of racing. A new round of lamenting at the pass to which international racing had come was appearing in the public press. It was widely felt that it would indeed be a good thing to discontinue the international event and for Gloucester to stage its own races. It was further recalled how well handled the recent

Anniversary Race had been in which elaborate rules were purposely omitted, being strictly boat for boat with thirty-man crews "engaged in or identified with the fishing industry."

Any likelihood of holding the Gloucester elimination race on October 12 now seemed remote. The *Henry Ford* and the *Elizabeth Howard* had returned to fishing and most certainly would not be back in time, and *Columbia*, pending outcome of the dispute, had merely remained at the wharf instead of proceeding with hull repairs. Ben wasn't sure whether to prepare for fishing or racing. When word finally came that *Columbia* was eligible, he filed a formal entry with the American committee and started at once to get her ready, first discharging the load of salt in the hold and replacing it with ballast.

On Monday morning, October 8, *Columbia* was hauled on Parkhurst railways. A good sized crowd of skippers and fishermen lined the narrow pier to watch her rise from the water. While on the ways it was planned to clean and paint the whole outside of the hull and to repair the shoe and the rudder, both damaged in launching. There were also certain repairs pursuant to the collision that the carpenters had not been able to accomplish with the vessel afloat. Upon coming off the ways a few days later she seemed a different boat. Gone were the scars of the collision and a summer's fishing and gone were the light gray topsides. She was shiny black now, in accordance with convention. Back in the water and with the rest of her new canvas bent on she took on the look of the lovely lady she was. An innovation in her racing rigging was the double set of staysail halyards devised by Ben Pine. It was possible with these to shift the fisherman's staysail from windward to leeward in tacking without dropping it all the way down to the deck as was previously necessary. It was expected that this would prove to be a time-saver in racing. As she lay at the Atlantic Supply Co. wharf she was joined there by *Elizabeth Howard*, home again and herself now getting ready for some racing. Both vessels anxiously awaited the early return of Captain Morrissey and the *Henry Ford* to make the elimination race a three-cornered affair and to give the *Ford* a fair chance to compete again with *Bluenose*—which, by the way, was to be the Canadian defender, the elimination race there having been called off for lack of any other entries.

When it became apparent that *Henry Ford* would not be home in time to participate in an October 12 elimination race, the American committee requested and was granted a postponement to October 27 of the Halifax races. This enabled *Columbia* to complete her preparations and still left time to engage her "trial horse," *Elizabeth Howard*, in a practice race, although from a business point of view it meant a delay in a planned winter freighting trip to Newfoundland for a load of herring. On Thursday, October 18, the two vessels went out off the "back shore" of Cape Ann to test the breeze. Ben Pine was in *Columbia* and Capt. Harry Gillie in the *Howard*, dubbed the "White Ghost" after her white topsides. A smart breeze was blowing about fifteen miles per hour from the northeast, making an excellent opportunity to see what the vessels, especially *Columbia*, would do. Since *Howard* was without her fore topmast, Ben, in fairness, reduced his sail correspondingly, although he was primarily interested in the distribution of his ballast. Moving the combined group of crew and guests, about forty people, back and forth on the deck indicated how the vessel would respond to various distributions of weight. As a result of the testing they moved a portion of the iron ballast forward, making *Columbia* much livelier. As to her sailing, she was very quick in stays, pointed well and seemed, they said, "stiff as a church." Although the *Howard* that day under Captain Gillie showed herself to be a great sticker, it was obvious that *Columbia* had the advantage in all points of sailing. With Capt. Charlie Harty and designer Burgess aboard as advisers, Ben tried setting everything to see how she would respond. With a burst of speed she walked right away from the *Howard*. Later, with corresponding rigs, the two vessels engaged in a lively brush on the way home, each doing his best to outwit the other. Finally coming from behind and passing his rival, Ben again set everything as he came into the outer harbor. All pronounced it to have been a very fruitful experience.

With preparation under way aboard *Columbia*, the committee had its own work to do. Perhaps most important was the raising of a war chest of $2,000 to defray expenses of the challenger in making those preparations. Although a good skipper and a good sport, Ben was not hesitant in passing his bills along to the committee, and it took some scratching to keep ahead of him. The committee voted to recommend the nomination of Frank C. Pearce of the Frank C. Pearce Company and Collector of the Port of Boston W. W. Lufkin from Essex to be the American representatives on the International Race Committee. Governor Cox of Massachusetts was asked to name Capt. George H. Peeples as the official representative of the state and Mayor William J. MacInnis of Gloucester was named the representative of the city. It was arranged that the official party would leave for Halifax aboard the U.S.S. *Bushnell* on Wednesday, October 24.

On the day that *Columbia* and *Elizabeth Howard* went out for their spin the *Henry Ford* arrived home from the banks. With a big trip of fish in the hold, no topmast rigged, and a crew and vessel tired from fishing, Captain Morrissey was something less than enthusiastic about racing that weekend. It was his opinion, he said, that *Columbia* should go to Halifax. After a conference with Ben Pine and the committee, he agreed nevertheless to give it a try and do what he could to get his vessel ready, even offering the help of himself and his crew to get the fish out. The fish were sold to Frank Pearce, who said he would be willing to pay overtime to discharge the trip. They worked all day Friday and most of Friday night to do it, and on Saturday took the *Ford* over and stepped her topmasts. Clayt felt there was neither a need nor time to have his vessel hauled. It was mutually agreed to race the three vessels on Sunday, with the winner to be declared the American challenger.

It was a poor day for racing on Sunday, but the three schooners set out anyway over the thirty-one-mile course, the committee following in the *Bushnell*. Columbia was obviously the superior boat, leading all the way. With the time limit of five and one-half hours expired and *Columbia* still six and one-half miles from the finish, it was the unanimous decision of the committee that *Columbia* be named the American challenger. They could hardly have decided otherwise. At the last buoy she had led the *Henry Ford* by nearly 19 minutes and the *Elizabeth Howard* by 26.

Amid a rousing send-off from a large crowd assembled on the Atlantic Supply Co. wharf the next afternoon, *Columbia* cast off at 2:15 for Halifax. Last to leave the ship was Mayor MacInnis, who led the crowd in a hearty cheer for the vessel and her skipper. After a tow from the tug *Mariner* she was left off at Ten Pound Island where, with all canvas set and the Stars and Stripes at her peak, she sailed for the open sea.

The shouts and farewells had hardly more than died away when with a sickening thump she fetched over a ledge outside Great Round Rock off the breakwater. A hurried examination below showed no apparent damage and there were no signs of leaking, but as a precaution it was felt advisable to turn back and have the vessel hauled out. So, after a voyage of one hour, she was back at the dock. With each of Gloucester's six railways momentarily occupied they felt it best to wait until morning and take the ways about to be vacated by the *Elsie*. This was done and it was found that about five feet of shoe was badly splintered. Working in a pouring rain and gale which ordinarily would have suspended yard operations, the carpenters actually replaced twelve feet of shoe and on Wednesday morning *Columbia* was launched again. Inasmuch as the gale was still blowing in Gloucester and blowing still harder off shore, *Columbia* prudently waited out the storm. Thus at 9:10 on Thursday morning with Ben Pine at the wheel she cast off once more and under her own sail beat down the harbor on her way to Halifax. This time her departure was more subdued. She met the *Bushnell* in the outer harbor and together they passed out to sea. Off Thatcher's each ship took its own course, to be rejoined at Halifax. Aboard the *Bushnell* was the official United States party and guests, including Selectman Frank McKenzie of Essex, State Senator John A. Stoddart representing the Commonwealth of Massachusetts, noted marine photographer Albert Cook Church, Mayor MacInnis and International Committeeman W. W. Lufkin, who was also delegated to be the official representative of President Coolidge.

The President had wired Mr. Lufkin of his interest in the races and expressed himself as gratified by the public enthusiasm. He extended his greetings to the participants and hoped for a fine display of sportsmanship.

Aboard *Columbia* were thirty Gloucestermen determined to make every effort humanly possible to beat the *Bluenose* and return the Dennis Trophy to that window on Main Street where it had been placed three years earlier by Marty Welch and the men of *Esperanto*. Here is the list of the men who hoped to do it:

Capt. Simon Theriault	Arthur Gillie
Capt. Daniel Nelson	George Roberts
Capt. Henry Langworthy	William Keating
Capt. Harry Gillie	Alphonse Boudrow
Capt. Stephen Post	Charles Amero
Capt. Jack Sparrow	Thomas Smith
Capt. Colin Powers	Charles Dagle
Capt. William Clancy	Alexander Chisolm
Capt. James Gannon	Burns Benham
Capt. Daniel McDonald	Charles Martell
Capt. Almon Malloch	Charles Martell, Jr.
Mickey Hall	Capt. Ben Pine
William E. McDonald	

Writer James B. Connolly, a friend of Ben Pine, was along for the ride, as was designer Starling Burgess and Columbia Associate Kenneth J. Ferguson.

6 ★ The Series of 1923

Shortly before midnight of Friday, October 26, the *Columbia* reached Halifax after a run of thirty-eight hours, tying up at Pickford and Black's wharf. For the most part the passage had been a good one with a fair breeze of wind. To quote her passenger, James B. Connolly, "She logged mile after mile at better than a fourteen-knot clip, and through it all she never more than put her quarter scuppers one plank under." He went on to say that "she waltzed along so smoothly that the gang playing cards below, seated on bait boxes in the open spaces of the cabin floor, did not even have to brace their feet to hold their seats." In fact, he waxed positively lyrical as he spoke of *Columbia* having "poetry of motion, speed, beauty and stiffness." Nevertheless, it was the trip to Halifax that indicated to Ben Pine that all was not quite what it should be regarding *Columbia*'s steering. Captain Geele had tried to tell him this, but Ben had merely shrugged it off.

There had been a strong fair wind for most of the trip, but inside Sambro, as they neared the approach to Halifax harbor, the wind grew still stronger and hauled ahead, and she found herself beating her way to the harbor against a real hard gale. There had been nothing noticeably wrong a week ago when she was out on her spin with *Elizabeth Howard*, and she had acted all right in the light airs of Sunday's race with the *Henry Ford*, but tonight she seemed to have trouble coming about, and at one point, standing in towards the rocks of Chebucto Head, there was concern that she wouldn't make it in time. Obviously something was wrong. Some thought that possibly the fact that the mainmast had a rather pronounced rake might have something to do with it, but Ben felt it was more probable that she needed greater rudder area. He resolved to try and do something about this if the opportunity presented itself.

The *Bluenose* had arrived from *Lunenburg* on Thursday night. Because of the thick weather outside and lack of wind in the inner harbor she was brought to Plant's wharf by a tug. Taking advantage of the interim, she went out on Friday to make a practice run over the course. As she returned to harbor in the afternoon she fell in with the *Bushnell* just arriving from Gloucester and easily maintained the *Bushnell*'s twelve-knot speed. It appeared to knowledgeable observers on *Bushnell* that she was noticeably lighter than she had been in last year's contest, seeming to be quite tender and scuppering freely. Such indeed was the case, for designer Roué felt that she had been too deep last year and had reduced the ballast in *Bluenose* from 110 to about 90 tons. His principal concern was that she would still have ballast enough to do well to windward in a smart breeze. Today's trial had been chiefly to determine a proper trim.

In a situation somewhat like the year before at Gloucester when the welcoming committee had been "caught short," the *Bushnell* with her load of dignitaries arrived at her pier about an hour early, catching the Canadians napping. They quickly recovered, however, and with Premier Armstrong of Nova Scotia as the spokesman, extended a cordial and hearty welcome to W. W. Lufkin and the American delegation, who, if the truth be known, were not a bit unhappy to be stepping ashore. After being engulfed in the utter miseries of seasickness aboard the *Bushnell* as she rolled her way across the bounding Bay of Fundy in the tail-end of Wednesday's gale, they were all still a little green at that point. But they soon regained their equilibrium and their composure and were happily swept into a round of welcoming hospitality and social events of all kinds.

When it had become apparent to the American committee that because of the accident and the storm *Columbia* would be delayed in leaving Gloucester, they had requested that the first race be moved from Saturday to Monday. The Trustees granted this request and thus there was time for *Columbia* to catch her breath as it were and get set for the first contest. An interval before racing was required as well to provide an opportunity to make the official measurements of the hulls of each vessel. This was done on Saturday morning with *Bluenose* being measured first. Taking the official measurements was R. J. Milgate accompanied by designers Roué and Burgess for the United States. As soon as they had finished with *Bluenose*, Captain Walters availed himself of the fine northwest breeze and took his vessel out for a second practice run. Turning now to *Columbia*, the measurer decided that it was too rough to measure her where she was, making it necessary to move the vessel to another wharf where the water was smoother. Her waterline measured exactly 110 feet and her "racing length" (length of hull) was determined by Mr. Milgate to be 141 feet 2½ inches.

In accepting *Columbia*'s eligibility for competition the Trustees had based their judgment on the plans and dimensions of Starling Burgess as submitted by Ben Pine. However, *Columbia*'s arrival afforded Captain Walters an opportunity to look her over and compare her with his own vessel as they lay at neighboring wharves. By Sunday he began to protest to the Trustees that he did not believe the figures, expressing doubt about the stated displacement and draft. It looked to him, he said, that *Columbia* was as burdensome as *Bluenose*, although there was considerable difference in their dimensions. Accordingly he demanded that *Columbia* be put on the ways for measurement, recalling as he did so the way in which the Americans had made him haul out in the 1921 series with *Elsie* and again last year in the series with *Henry Ford*. While he was at it, he reiterated his demand of the past week that the time limit for the races be reduced from six hours to five, and then for good measure suggested that if they were measuring, they might like to measure *Columbia*'s mainsail, which was known to have stretched a little coming up from Gloucester. This all seemed strange, for only Friday Angus been quoted as saying: "Piney is a fine fellow, square as a brick—and a true sportsman!"

The Trustees duly considered the charges brought by Captain Walters and concluded that the dimensions supplied on the plans were satisfactory, and unless Captain Walters wished to file a formal complaint, they would not require *Columbia* to haul out before racing. In conferences with Captain Walters and Captain

Pine they suggested as a compromise that if *Columbia* won the first race or won the series, she would be asked to haul out for measurement. In the matter of the time limit, they decided it should remain at six hours, while the measurements of *Columbia's* mainsail were found to be within the rule.

Captain Pine was obviously annoyed by all this, believing all along that his vessel was well within the regulations, but rather than aggravate the controversy, he agreed to the arrangement, and Captain Walters in turn consented to let *Columbia* race. The vessel, meanwhile, as she lay at her wharf was visited by throngs of sightseers come to see the lovely challenger and to speculate on her capabilities. A Halifax policeman was detailed aboard to keep the crowd moving. Many affirmed their belief that she was a winner. One man claimed to have $4,000 to wager on the Yankee but couldn't place it; "she's got Nova Scotia that scared," he said. It was felt that Ben Pine had an able crew, of whom a great many were Nova Scotians and Newfoundlanders, and also he had plenty of smart advice in the eleven skippers among them. (Of course, these didn't quite measure up to the twenty-six captains in the *Bluenose* crew of thirty.) At any rate Ben and his crew took advantage of the only opportunity they had to try out before the start and went out on Sunday afternoon for a little spin; with hardly a breath of air stirring she gave a good account of herself as a drifter in the confines of the outer harbor.

On Monday morning *Columbia* was the first to make sail, leaving Pickford and Black's wharf at 8:00 A.M. beneath a leaden and showery sky. Both vessels were at the line marked by the flagstaff on the Halifax breakwater well before the nine o'clock starting gun. In spite of the showers an enormous crowd was gathered about the adjacent headlands and occupied every vantage point along the shore. Afloat, scores of pleasure craft hovered around. The wind was from the west and though less than twelve miles per hour was increasing in velocity. The committee, therefore, signalled for the sailing of course number two. This meant that it would be south 6.3 miles from the line to the Inner Automatic; southeast 6.4 miles to the Southeast Automatic; southwest 9.6 miles to Sambro gas buoy; northeast 11.25 miles to the Inner Automatic again and north 6.3 miles to the finish, a total of 39.85 miles.

It should be stated here as a matter of academic interest that with particular regard to the performance of each boat, it is difficult to determine exactly what happened throughout each of the races. From a careful study of seven printed accounts of these races, no two of which are in complete agreement, plus interviews with the only member of *Columbia*'s crew remaining alive, it would appear that there were as many versions of the events as there were observers. In relating the conduct of the racing we will endeavor, therefore, to record what appears to be a consensus of fact and to interpret the printed accounts with the benefit of hindsight.

With a little time to spare before the gun both schooners sailed a short stretch out along the course to test the wind. The five-minute warning found both again well back of the line and some distance apart with *Bluenose* in the windward position. At the gun *Bluenose* had come about and was making for the line, with *Columbia* just turning after failing in a maneuver to gain a starting advantage. *Bluenose* crossed with about a five length or 30 second lead. It was a close reach for the 6.3 miles to the first mark, with *Bluenose* establishing an increasing lead over the challenger, leading by 1 minute 16 seconds as they rounded the Inner Automatic. The time: *Bluenose* 9.35.30; *Columbia* 9.36.46. From here it was another reach of 6.4 miles to the Southeast Automatic and *Bluenose* continued to build her lead, rounding the buoy 2 minutes 17 seconds ahead of *Columbia*. The time: *Bluenose* 10.06.43; *Columbia* 10.09.00. The wind was now beginning to back more to the southwest and the next leg would be almost a dead beat to windward for a distance of 9.4 miles to the Sambro gas buoy. Although the *Bluenose* had very definitely outsailed her rival in the first two legs, *Columbia* on the windward leg began to give a better account of herself. She demonstrated a positive ability to point higher than *Bluenose* and appeared to be footing quite as fast. The only tack in the entire race was made on this leg, with *Columbia* coming about in approximately one quarter the time taken by *Bluenose*, a fact occasioned in

105

large measure by the ability to reset the staysail without dropping it to the deck.

Both vessels began the leg with a long starboard tack out to sea. The wind was increasing somewhat and was taking the tops off the lumpy seas, making for smoother water. In this situation *Columbia* was at her best and began to gain on the defender. *Bluenose* was first to come about with *Columbia* immediately following, she being to windward of *Bluenose*. As they approached the buoy on the port tack, Captain Walters appeared to misjudge his distance and overstood the mark, allowing *Columbia* to round the buoy with a 15 second lead. Time: *Columbia* 12.03.15; *Bluenose* 12.03.30.

From here it was to be a very broad reach to the northeast of 11.25 miles back to the Inner Automatic. There now ensued a long series of luffs with Captain Pine struggling to maintain his slight advantage and Captain Walters attempting to come up and gain a weather berth. With every luff *Bluenose* would come up until her bowsprit was almost even with the end of *Columbia's* main boom only to get a bit of back wind and drop astern. For eight miles they did this, the maneuvers carrying the two vessels far in towards the shore. While thus engaged they found themselves approaching the buoy marking the rocks of Bell Shoal, which projected well to the eastward of Chebucto Head. Onward they pressed with *Columbia* edging *Bluenose* further up to the weather. The Canadian pilot aboard the *Columbia* warned Ben to keep to seaward of the buoy, which he did, but Angus held his position and kept doggedly on, and as the buoy was reached, passed through the green water inside the mark with *Columbia* close on the outside. While doing this, *Bluenose* finally succeeded in luffing up across *Columbia's* stern, at which point she immediately bore off, dousing her staysail and swinging her foresail wing and wing. *Columbia* was completely blanketed, virtually stopping dead in her tracks. As the *Bluenose* passed, her main boom was so close aboard *Columbia* as to strike the main port shrouds, smashing the sheerpoles and scraping forward till it fouled in *Columbia's* jib downhaul, catching there for a couple of minutes and creating the illusion that *Columbia* was being

106

towed. In the process, *Bluenose*'s boom came unshipped and a mighty effort was required of the *Bluenose*'s crew to fleet it back in place.

This appeared to decide the race, for with only her mainsail drawing while all others were deprived of wind, *Columbia* settled back while *Bluenose*, again with everything set, pulled out ahead and on to the next mark, which she rounded with a comfortable lead of 1 minute 1 second. Time: *Bluenose* 1.12.44; *Columbia* 1.13.46. In effect the contest was over now as *Bluenose* on the six mile broad reach to the line held her margin, even adding a few seconds to it as each vessel tore off the remaining few miles to the finish. Thus was *Bluenose* the winner in the first race by 1 minute 20 seconds. Time: *Bluenose* 1.43.42; *Columbia* 1.45.02. Now it was time for the post-mortems.

In regard to the sailing qualities and abilities of the schooners it was obvious that as far as this race was concerned, *Bluenose* held the advantage in all points of sailing, except the ability to point. In a beat to windward *Columbia* was definitely able to point higher and to foot as fast as *Bluenose*. In tacking, she also showed an ability to come about much faster. Here it was a combination of being naturally quicker in stays than *Bluenose* and having a crew able to perform their functions faster (with an assist from Ben Pine's set of double staysail halyards). *Columbia* gave evidence, however, of being too heavily ballasted, and it was becoming more evident she was not steering as she should. There were times when it was difficult to hold her to her course, creating the impression in the minds of some observers that she was having an unnecessarily rough time of it. The blame, it was felt, lay in what was termed "a miscalculation of the builder" in making the rudder too small. In short, *Columbia* had not been at her best.

The fouling by *Bluenose* was something else again, and the impression one gets of the incident depends upon which account is to be believed. That *Columbia* had been fouled was obvious from the damage she sustained. With both vessels back at their wharves, the friends and supporters of each crowded around to hear the stories of what had happened. In discussing the event it might be useful to preface any remarks by quoting from a section of the rules dealing with such a situation:

"When a vessel is approaching a shore, shoal, rock, vessel or other dangerous obstruction and cannot go clear by altering her course without fouling another vessel, then the latter shall, on being hailed by the former, at once give room. In case one vessel is forced to tack or to bear away in order to give room, the other shall also tack or bear away as the case may be at as near the same time as is possible without danger of fouling." Nothing in the rules prevented a vessel from sailing in any waters desired by the helmsman.

It was the claim of Captain Walters that *Columbia* had crowded him into the dangerous waters to the point where he was forced to bear off. Before doing so he hailed the *Columbia* to bear away and give him sea room. Instead of bearing away, *Columbia* instead further crowded him on the wrong side of the buoy and luffed into him. Witnesses said that as they approached Bell Rock buoy their pilot shouted to the helmsman, Capt. Albert Himmelman, to bear away. "Bear away and we strike him!" Himmelman shouted back. "Strike him or strike the rocks!" the pilot answered. At this point *Bluenose* swung, with Captain Pine still trying to luff.

Aboard the *Columbia* it was a different story. Captain Pine contended that what had happened was deliberate on the part of Angus Walters. Knowing that there was ample water on the wrong side of the buoy, he had taken a short cut through it in an avowed attempt to create a blanket and gain the advantage. Moreover, Ben claimed that at no time did anyone aboard *Columbia* hear a hail from the *Bluenose*. Therefore, hearing no hail, he was perfectly justified in maintaining his course. Had not the *Bluenose* scraped out ahead, he felt *Columbia* would have won. The crewmen on *Columbia* were convinced that the Canadian pilot aboard their boat told Ben to go on the correct side of the buoy in order to give *Bluenose* the opportunity to create a blanket.

Captain Pine, however, was strongly urged by many supporters and especially by his crew to file a formal protest with

108

the sailing committee in connection with the fouling. It was felt that this was unquestionably a violation of the rules of any race, as indeed it probably was. After carefully weighing the situation, Captain Pine concluded he would waive his right of protest, feeling that to protest would only serve to exacerbate an already delicate situation. A protest, if allowed, would have given him the race, but would have tapped a reservoir of ill feeling. No doubt he also had in mind that if it came to a showdown before the committee as to where the fault lay, it would be a case of "six of one and half-a-dozen of the other." When asked by a reporter that afternoon what he intended to do, Ben shrugged and replied, "We'll be nearer the starting gun tomorrow than we were today."

When tomorrow came, the weather was flat calm and thick-of-fog. The committee called for first one then two postponements, but no improvement was forthcoming, so the race was put over until Wednesday. Immediately taking advantage of the hiatus, Ben Pine set about doing something to improve *Columbia's* steering. The night before, Ben had engaged a diver with the thought he might be able to go down and spike another piece to the trailing edge of the rudder blade to give it more area. The diver appeared in the morning and was about to go to work when a representative of the Trustees appeared in the person of H. R. Silver, who tactfully suggested that with the series underway, such a move would be "unwise." Ben made the comment to a reporter's question later in the day, "They wouldn't let me do it." He was able, however, to shift a portion of her ballast forward to improve the trim.

Having decided to defer the second race until Wednesday, the sailing committee repaired to the rooms of the Royal Nova Scotia Yacht Squadron, where they took up the matters of Monday's race. Of most importance, they decided that henceforth any buoy marking shoal waters was to be passed on the seaward side. They were unanimous in their decision that they wanted no more incidents of boats being crowded into shoal waters with its attendant danger to the safety of ship and crew. Also, while Ben Pine had not protested the fouling by *Bluenose,* he and his crew

had vigorously protested against the Canadian observer on
Columbia, one C. H. J. Snider, a Toronto newspaper man. He
had been making photographs and taking copious notes during
Monday's race and his account in the morning paper infuriated
Columbia's crew. The committee heard the evidence and sus-
tained the protest, designating P. K. Wade, also of Toronto, to
take Snider's place. Lastly, they ruled for a second time that
Columbia need not be hauled out for measurement.

In the afternoon, while *Bluenose* remained at the wharf, Ben
took *Columbia* out for a spin. The fog had lifted and a little
breeze had sprung up so they went out along the course a short
way, running off some practice in tacking. From full away on
one tack to full away on the other was taking 40 seconds. (Before
coming to Halifax *Columbia* was reported to have done the same
thing off Cape Ann in less than 20 seconds.) Captain Pine
seemed pleased with the change of trim produced by moving
his ballast. They were accompanied on the run by their Canadian observer, who was along to make sure that none of that
ballast went overboard. Back at the wharf that evening three
Halifax policemen came aboard and stood guard all night as
insurance that the ballast would have a comfortable night's rest.

Early Wednesday morning seemed hardly more promising as
a racing day than Tuesday had been, with sky dark and rain coming down in torrents, but it let up about eight o'clock, and with
some suggestion of a breeze the vessels went out to the line.
Signals were set for course number four which made for a six
mile run to the Inner Automatic; an eleven mile reach to Shutin
Island Buoy; a nine mile close reach to the Outer Automatic
and a thirteen mile beat to the finish.

At the fifteen-minute gun both schooners were jockeying for
position. As he said he would be, Ben was nearer the line at
the starting gun but still Angus beat him to it, crossing with a
10 second lead although Columbia had a little more headway.
As expected, the race soon developed into a luffing match with
first one vessel and then the other gaining a brief advantage.
It was listless going, with the wind seeming to pick up a little
only to die away, the predicted gale never materializing. There

was lively work aboard both craft as they jibed and shifted sail to follow up the slightest advantage of wind or position. At length *Columbia* managed to work herself into the lead and rounded the first mark 1 minute 24 seconds ahead of *Bluenose*. Time: *Columbia* 10.29.20; *Bluenose* 10.30.44. It had been an hour and a half to cover six miles.

From this point on, *Columbia* slowly increased her margin over *Bluenose*. The weather was drizzly and a little squall went by but the wind never really increased much over five or six knots. With a little over half the distance to the second mark covered, *Columbia* established a lead of about three-quarters of a mile which she held to the buoy. Time: *Columbia* 12.24.25; *Bluenose* 12.28.36. With three and one-half hours gone by, the vessels had covered a mere seventeen miles of the thirty-nine-mile course; obviously they would never finish in time. With the winds still light and the relative positions of the two schooners unchanged, the committee called the whole thing off at two o'clock, and the schooners headed for home. Almost as if on signal a smart breeze sprang up, creating the only excitement of the day as the two vessels decided to have it out on the run back to Halifax. Swinging along smartly now, *Bluenose* overhauled her rival and swept into the harbor with a good lead, achieving at least a moral victory of sorts for her day's efforts.

With a little spare time on his hands and perhaps from having had the embarrassment of trailing *Columbia* in the official racing, Angus Walters once more complained about the *Columbia*, saying he was still not satisfied with the figures taken from the blueprints. He thought *Columbia* seemed lighter in today's race than she had on Monday and felt something must be wrong. He intimated that his crew would refuse to race any more until *Columbia* was put on the ways. He was quoted as saying, "We agreed to sail against *Columbia* on Monday provided the schooner was put on the ways for measurements the same day if she won, or on the first occasion when there was a day in which no race was sailed. Instead of attending to this yesterday, Captain Pine went out cruising over the course after the committee had called a postponement."

Captain Pine, when he heard of Walters' statement, replied, "It would be to our advantage if *Columbia* went on the ways. We could then dump out some of the excess ballast we are carrying. [*Columbia* was reported to be carrying 120 tons of pig iron, boiler punchings and cement.] Our water line is 110 feet when it should be 108 and we're only carrying canvas for the 108 foot figure. From the start *Columbia* has been ready to go on the ways. The committee wanted us to race on Monday. It was agreed that if we won that day, we should immediately be taken out of the water. We lost instead. According to our interpretation of the committee's ruling there was no need of hauling *Columbia* in that event. We will abide by any ruling made. Certainly we have no fear of having *Columbia* measured now or any time."

(Note: The rules entitled a schooner to a sail area equal to 80% of the square of the waterline length expressed in square feet. For a waterline of 110 feet *Columbia* was entitled to a sail area of 9,680 square feet. For a waterline of 108 feet *Columbia* would have been entitled to a sail area of 9,333 square feet. It was reported before the races that her sail area was 9,250 square feet and, if this was correct, was thus 430 square feet less than that to which she was legally entitled. *Bluenose* with a waterline of 112 square feet was entitled to a sail area of 10,035 square feet. It was reported that she was carrying 9,999 square feet. *Columbia* was figured to have a displacement of 269.6 long tons to 280 long tons for *Bluenose*.)

Whether the International Committee took Ben at his word or were only weary of all the discussion is not recorded. At any rate they elected to let matters stand and did not request *Columbia* to be hauled out. Therefore at nine o'clock on Thursday morning the schooners appeared at the line for the third time.

Although still mostly overcast from the heavy rain of the previous night, there was every indication that the weather would be ideal for racing. The wind was blowing from the northeast at an 18 knot clip and increasing, with patches of blue sky beginning to show. It promised to produce the kind of race that everyone had been looking for. The sailing committee signalled that course number two, the same as Monday's, would be followed. Today with northeast winds it would mean a six mile reach from the line to the Inner Automatic; a run of nine and a half miles to Sambro gas buoy and a beat of seventeen miles back to the finish by way of the Inner Automatic.

The fifteen-minute gun found both schooners maneuvering in the cove back of the breakwater which marked the line. With *Columbia* in the advance, *Bluenose* was duplicating her every move. At 5 minutes, both were on the starboard tack with everything set except the fore gaff topsails, the *Columbia* close-hauled heading up the harbor and *Bluenose*, sheets eased, idling down the line. At 2 minutes, *Columbia* squared away and headed for the line, with *Bluenose* coming about a moment later and crossing the line 13 seconds ahead and to weather of the challenger. Angus had done it again. Time: *Bluenose* 9.00.27; *Columbia* 9.00.40.

Immediately it became a contest, with the schooners running almost before the wind as they scudded along for the first mark. In a few minutes *Columbia* brought herself up and almost a length ahead of her rival, only to have *Bluenose* catch a puff and again surge into the lead, going about a quarter mile to weather of *Columbia*. Ben took in his sheets and set out to gain the weather position for himself, with *Bluenose* then in the lead by several lengths. At 9:20, with *Bluenose* leading by about 55 seconds, they came upon Lighthouse Bank buoy, which *Bluenose* passed on the inside while *Columbia*, in accordance with regulations, passed to seaward. Shortly *Columbia* bore off and it appeared that Ben had abandoned his attempt to weather the defender. *Bluenose*, the while, was increasing her lead and rounded the mark with a margin of 1 minute 49 seconds. Time: *Bluenose* 9.44.21; *Columbia* 9.46.10.

By now the wind was up to twenty-five knots and the big two-stickers, carrying all the canvas they owned, were plunging into the oncoming seas at better than fourteen knots, leaving *Lady Laurier*, the press boat, herself steaming at twelve knots, and others of the spectator fleet far behind. *Columbia's* long lean bow was splitting the seas and throwing great sheets of green water into the air on either side while the high full bow of the *Bluenose* sent tons of water thundering off to leeward as she plunged. Altogether it was a marine spectacle such as had seldom been witnessed before.

Perhaps because she tended to slice the waves more than throw them off, *Columbia* was taking a great deal of water over the deck. At one point a boarding sea swept crewman Capt. Stephen Post into the lee scuppers, where he was washed aft and about to go over the side when grabbed by five of his shipmates, who managed to drag him out and up onto the cabin trunk. Also, with ballast shifted forward as they had done on Tuesday, *Columbia*, under conditions like this, was a little heavy by the head, giving her a tendency to root. For much of the second and third legs it took two men to hold the wheel and keep her to it. Topping off this bucket of worms was the staysail, which at one point became either jammed or tangled somehow in the springstay so that they had to drop it and set it several times before it was correctly secured.

On the second leg *Columbia* ate up some of the distance between the two vessels, gaining back some 20 seconds by the time they reached the second mark. Here, in a display of courage and seamanship of heroic proportions, both vessels jibed around the buoy, each skipper handling with consummate skill as he did so over 9,000 square feet of canvas hung on sticks nearly 120 feet tall and under tons of pressure. Happily for all concerned the gear held. *Columbia*, more than *Bluenose*, rolled down with a shudder, but quickly recovered and with staysails "scandalized" (dropped about one half from normal position), both vessels ran off wing and wing for the third mark. Time: *Bluenose* 10.16.10, *Columbia* 10.17.39, for a difference now of 1 minute 29 seconds.

Indomitably they plunged along, rolling booms under as the puffs hit them. *Columbia* now developed a problem here, too, for she dipped her boom frequently to the point where it hampered her steering. There had not been a proper chance to stretch and re-cut her new mainsail before coming to Halifax and now she was paying for it. Even taking up on the topping lift did not seem to help. In spite of all her troubles she continued to gain ever so slowly on *Bluenose* and had reduced the defender's lead by another 9 seconds at the third mark. Time: *Bluenose* 11.15.03; *Columbia* 11.16.23.

Here began the long seventeen-mile thresh back to the finish line, and both schooners went to work with a vengeance in near gale winds which now approached thirty knots, still increasing. Before rounding the last mark Angus had doused his fore gaff topsail and was not to handle sail again until nearly home. Ben, however, kept his on as both vessels started the leg on a starboard tack. It stayed up for about fifteen minutes when, with *Columbia* obviously having trouble holding her course, they attempted to bring it in. For some reason they couldn't handle it properly and it sagged off to leeward for a long time before being clewed up, all of which caused *Columbia* to begin falling behind.

In justice, all of the trouble was not confined to the *Columbia*, for during this leg the main topmast backstay on the *Bluenose* parted at the spreader. It came within inches of A. P. Loring, the American observer on *Bluenose*, as it fell and caught Captain Walters across the arm as he crouched at the wheel. They say he never even flinched.

Essentially it can be said that these last two windward legs determined the race. Try as he might, Ben Pine and his *Columbia* were unable to overtake the *Bluenose*, which settled into a comfortable lead and was not to be headed. At one point off Ketch Harbor, well up toward the Inner Automatic, *Columbia* seemed to come alive and set a tremendous pace, pointing as she should and threatening to close the half-mile gap between herself and *Bluenose*. Angus would not be outfoxed, however, and when Ben broke out his staysail again to gain a little more speed, Angus did too. The trouble was that once more *Columbia's* staysail fouled; she lost rather than gained. Ben tried splitting tacks to gain a little ground; it didn't work. A favorable spot of wind allowed him to save a hitch over *Bluenose*; it wasn't enough. Whatever Ben tried, Angus was there ahead of him.

Because of the constant tacking and maneuvering, it was impossible to take the official time at the last mark, so the committee boat went on to the finish line to await the result. With squalls of rain and snow slanting over the sea, the *Bluenose* came up the harbor to cross the line, winner by 2 minutes 45 seconds over *Columbia*. Time: *Bluenose* 2.36.03; *Columbia* 2.38.48.

With a second victory by their *Bluenose*, Halifax and Nova Scotia cut loose with wild jubilation. The series was over and Angus could once more stow the Dennis Trophy aboard his *Bluenose*, and head home to Lunenburg. Both vessels had given an excellent account of themselves and both had been sailed in a masterful fashion, the race being little short of an epic in the international fishermen's series.

The shrewdness, skill and acumen of Angus Walters as a sailing master was obvious and he was possessed of a vessel with extraordinary sailing and handling qualities. That she was as good as she was is attested by the number of times one finds the use of the word "freak" in reference to the *Bluenose* and her speed. Designer Roué was himself at a loss to explain exactly why she sailed so well. He had tried to design other schooners for various of his Canadian clients which would beat the *Bluenose*, but none was anywhere near as successful. (In the course of her career *Bluenose* was to sail in twenty-one official races, defeating fifteen different schooners and herself losing but six times.) With the high bow that Angus had given her, she was hardly the sleek and beautiful creature *Columbia* was, but for the Canadians it was "handsome is as handsome does." Not to be forgotten was the fact that she was a big vessel, and, to use the axiom we put forth in the opening pages of this narrative, "A good big vessel will beat a good smaller vessel, other conditions being equal." And here we saw it; a good *Bluenose* with a keen man like Angus for a skipper had beaten a good *Columbia* with a keen man like Ben Pine.

On the other hand the ability of *Columbia* was not to be underestimated. That she was an able vessel was beyond doubt, as evidenced by her performance of the past week. That she was far from being at her best was also beyond all doubt. From the

116

beginning she had been beset by a succession of difficulties, some rather minor and some of major concern. First and foremost was the persistent trouble with the steering. Some blamed it on trim; some on the size of the rudder; some to the rake of the mainmast. Nobody, apparently, considered the possibility of damage to the rudder stock. Then there was the question of ballast. Why Ben had put in so much is hard to say. If published figures are to be believed, she was carrying about thirty tons more ballast than the *Bluenose* and in a slightly smaller vessel. Under the rules it could not be taken out during the series but could only be shifted. This had been done, and it improved her performance in Wednesday's drifting match but was no good for Thursday's gale. She had a lot of trouble with her upper sails. On several occasions the fore gaff topsail and the staysail jammed somehow or caught as they were being set or taken in, requiring frantic corrective effort, serving in every case to slow the vessel. Here *Columbia* was not alone, for even Angus had difficulties with his headsails on one occasion. There were a number of incidents which plagued them, as when Captain Post nearly washed overboard and another occasion when Mickey Hall at the mast head caught his leg in the staysail sheet, nearly plunging to the deck.

On the positive side was a beautiful hull which every competent observer agreed was probably as fast as *Bluenose* if given a proper chance. In windward work the vessel had demonstrated a definite ability to outpoint her rival. In summary, it boiled down to the fact that there was really little to choose between in the two schooners or the ability of their masters, and that if *Columbia* had been tuned to the extent the *Bluenose* was, and had a crew as well drilled, the contest of the past week, close as it was, would have been even closer. No doubt *Columbia* received the highest tribute ever given her when, many years later in an interview on Canadian television, Captain Walters was asked the question, "What, in your opinion, is the best boat the Americans ever produced?" To this he replied without any hesitation, "The *Columbia*."

With the series concluded, a ceremonial farewell banquet to

honor the American visitors was planned by the Canadian officials for Thursday evening. Not planned was a meeting of the sailing committee hastily called early in the evening to consider a formal protest lodged against the *Bluenose* by Ben Pine in behalf of *Columbia*. The protest concerned the violation by *Bluenose* of the newly adopted special rule requiring racing participants to pass on the seaward side of any buoy marking shoal water. That morning, in an action clearly noted by all observers, the *Bluenose* had passed on the inside of Lighthouse Bank buoy, thus violating a rule not yet forty-eight hours old. The committee acknowledged receipt of the protest and at once summoned Captain Walters to offer an explanation. He readily admitted passing the buoy on the wrong side, saying only that he hadn't seen it in time to do otherwise.

If the authority of the committee and the rules were to be maintained, there was therefore no alternative but to disqualify the *Bluenose* on the grounds that she had not completed the official course in accordance with the sailing regulations. This was done and the race thereby was awarded to *Columbia*. The International Committee readily concurred in the action of the sailing committee, making the official announcement of the decision while the banquet was in progress. Needless to say, it had a rather sobering effect on the group gathered there in the hall and more particularly on the celebrants outside in the streets of Halifax.

Concurrently with the official announcement of *Bluenose's* disqualification, it was declared that the races now stood at one apiece and that the third race would be sailed at 9 A.M. on Saturday morning. It was felt that this would give *Bluenose* time to repair her topmast and backstay and perhaps to smooth troubled waters by having *Columbia* hauled for a draft measurement. How troubled the waters were came to light next morning when Angus announced that as far as he was concerned, the races were over and he and his men and his boat were going home. He would not, he said, abide by any decision such at that. In high dudgeon he argued that Lighthouse Bank buoy had been moved where it was as an examination stopmark in

World War I and did not indicate shoal water. Only if the committee would modify their ruling and call it "no race" would he stay. To its credit, however, the sailing committee was obdurate, holding steadfast to its decision.

At this, Captain Walters appealed to the International Committee. They, however, refused to consider the matter, saying that it was not a matter within their jurisdiction; that questions of this nature were wholly the province of the sailing committee; that if they said he was disqualified, he was disqualified.

For much of Friday morning the local group argued with Captain Walters, even Premier Armstrong attempting to dissuade him, all to no avail. He was not about to be deprived of his victory in any such fashion. At length they appealed to Arthur Zwicker, president of the Bluenose Corporation, to intervene in the interests of the national honor. This proved to be a tactical error, for Mr. Zwicker announced that if Angus and his crew went home, he would get another crew from Lunenburg to come over and sail the *Bluenose*. With that Captain Walters exercised his prerogative as skipper and managing owner and gave orders to cast off and head for Lunenburg. At two o'clock that afternoon the water boat *Defiance* arrived and towed the *Bluenose* out of Halifax harbor, thus ending any possibility that the series could be satisfactorily completed.

In the face of this *fait accompli* the International Committee was forced to cope with a wholly unexpected and difficult situation and one without precedent (although it had almost happened the year before). It was decided that if Ben Pine would appear at the line at nine o'clock the following morning and, in the absence of *Bluenose*, sail the *Columbia* over the course alone, he would be awarded the race and the series by default and would thereby be given the trophy. Ben was most emphatic in his refusal to do this, saying that he and his crew had no desire to take the trophy without winning it. He further announced that *Columbia* would, herself, leave for home in the morning. At this the International Committee again conferred and announced that, in view of the circumstances, the series of 1923 was hereby declared to be "unfinished," with the trophy remaining in the

119

custody of the Trustees. In the matter of prize money, they decided that the purse of $5,000 be divided in half, with $2,500 to be awarded immediately to the *Columbia* for expense money. Pending further decision, the remaining $2,500 was to be held by the committee.

That evening as the official American party prepared to board the *Bushnell* for the trip back to Gloucester, Mr. Lufkin, as head of the delegation, made a very gracious statement of thanks to the people of Halifax and of Nova Scotia for their wonderful hospitality and helpfulness, and expressed the feeling that all officials of the races from both countries had been eminently fair and had "moved every stone possible to avoid this unfortunate ending." It is certain he echoed the sentiments of many, for the present series at the official level had been characterized for the most part by an extraordinary atmosphere of cordiality and cooperation, a conscious effort, perhaps, to erase some of the rancor of 1922. From the beginning there had been a disposition on both sides to give and take in the interest of the sport. Great numbers of Canadians, that day, expressed an intense dismay and disappointment in the action of Captain Walters and his crew. There seemed to be a general feeling throughout Halifax at least that they were wrong in refusing to race. Some of the more outspoken went so far as to suggest that they should be barred from all future competition.

So, in an atmosphere of mixed emotion, Ben Pine and his men headed *Columbia* out of Halifax harbor at nine the next morning. In sudden startling contrast to the previous afternoon, when their own *Bluenose* had departed unnoticed and unsung, all Halifax cut loose with its horns and whistles in a spontaneous and heartwarming display of sportsmanship and good will toward their American guests. In a sense it was, perhaps, an attempt to apologize for the embarrassment they all felt in the actions of their countrymen. As for *Columbia*, she was pleased to be going home.

So quickly, it seemed, the whole business had exploded with a bang and was all over. The events of the past two days were on everyone's lips. It was astonishing how widespread and how

120

keen had been the interest in this series of races, and the manner in which it concluded was shocking to all. Of especial interest was the extent of the condemnation Captain Walters received in his own country. Canadians remained convinced that their *Bluenose* was a better vessel but the feeling was universal that, having committed a foul, he should have respected the ruling of the sailing committee and come back to race again.

The newspapers of Saturday and Sunday were full of editorial comment and evaluation of the affair. The *Moncton* (New Brunswick) *Transcript* hoped that the people of the United States would not look upon the skipper of the *Bluenose* as in any sense representing the sporting sentiment of Canada. In Halifax, the *Herald*, partisan to the core though it was, voiced editorial support of the committee in its ruling, although it felt that *Columbia*'s protest was based on "the merest kind of a technicality." It went on to say that *Columbia*'s chances were not materially injured nor were *Bluenose*'s chances bettered by what she had done. The *New York Times* called for Captain Walters to come back and race the *Columbia* again "for the sake of the honor of Canada." It pointed out that for a real and fair contest the rules must be heeded, recalling the words of Premier Armstrong at Thursday's banquet to the effect that an umpire's decision must be respected "no matter whose bows are stove." The *New York World*, with an article by its correspondent John B. Kelly, reviewed the remarkable similarity of Angus Walters' situation with that of Clayton Morrissey in 1922. It pointed out how Morrissey had taken everything handed to him and had still gone through with the show after supposedly winning two races. It felt that Captain Walters should have done the same.

All of this had its effect upon Captain Walters. He was a sensitive man, and with a couple of days for contemplation he decided that he had, indeed, made a grave mistake. Accordingly he sent a wire to H. R. Silver of the Trustees which read: "On reflection I regret the effects of my action. I was under a great strain. I am a fisherman, not a sportsman. I acted hurriedly and did not realize that so many other persons were so

121

keenly interested." He offered to race *Columbia* again if the committee wished him to.

If *Columbia* got a rousing send-off when she left Halifax, she got a bigger welcome when she arrived in Gloucester. At 9:20 on Monday morning her tall spars were sighted over the breakwater. Immediately the word spread like wildfire through the city. Everyone who could dropped whatever he was doing and headed for the waterfront. As she rounded the point of the breakwater she was met by Capt. Harry Clattenberg in the *Evelyn and Ralph*, who escorted her back into her berth at the Atlantic Supply Co. wharf. Coming past Ten-pound Island all hell broke loose. Every whistle, every horn, every bell—anything that would make a noise—let go with all it had. Booming over all was the mighty voice of the Gloucester fire whistle. Every vantage point was jammed—the Fort, Davis Brothers, every wharf, every place—while marching down from City Hall was the welcoming committee of city officials preceded by the High School R.O.T.C. band. For all Gloucester cared, she had won.

Columbia was dressed for the occasion with her own burgee, the Elks pennant and Old Glory at her mast head. As she approached the dock the band struck up "Yes, We Have No Bananas!" Then, as the lines hit the wharf, a rousing cheer went up from the crowd, the band playing "Hail, Hail, the Gang's All Here." At once an impromptu parade was organized, with the band leading the men of *Columbia* through the streets of Gloucester and back to the wharf. When at dinnertime it all finally petered out, Ben guessed that the time had come to go back fishing.

7 * The Middle Years

It was reminiscent of Cinderella coming home from the grand ball. At one moment here was *Columbia*, a beautiful princess, so to speak, with hordes of admirers crowding about to bask in her regal splendor and shout their acclaim; the next, a humble scullery maid back at her menial tasks. From queen of the fleet on November 5, *Columbia* found herself on November 6 being reduced to a herring freighter. It was fairly common in Gloucester in those days for vessels engaged in dory handlining to spend their winters freighting herring from Newfoundland, some of it pickled, most of it salt. The salt herring, a common staple of fish markets, especially in New England, was carried below in the hold in the same fashion as a regular trip of fish with the herring packed in layers of rock salt. The pickled herring, packed in great hogsheads of brine, were carried as a deck cargo. Many were the times when these deck cargoes were washed away by the heavy winter seas or were jettisoned to save the ship. On arrival in Gloucester, pickled herring was washed free of brine and smoked, to be used also as food fish (kippers). Vessels engaged in this work carried a crew of ten to twelve men and sailed under what was commonly referred to as "winter rig"; that is, they used only the four lower sails, with topmasts, topsails and staysails being taken out and put away.

So on Tuesday morning *Columbia* was at the Atlantic Maritime wharf having her topmasts taken out by rigger George Roberts. With things back to normal, they took eleven days to change the rigging, gather a crew and load stores. On Saturday, November 17, *Columbia*, now in command of Capt. Almon Malloch, sailed on her first herring trip to Newfoundland. Her departure was marked by a mere line in the shipping notices of the *Gloucester Daily Times*.

That same day a letter was received by the Trustees of the International Trophy from an attorney representing the owners of the schooner *Bluenose*. They were informed that said owners felt themselves to be legally entitled to the trophy and the prize money and that unless the same were handed over immediately, the matter would be taken to the courts. It was variously reported from Halifax that the International Committee was reluctant to give Captain Walters a penny and that the Trustees were adamant in refusing to award him the trophy.

On the 12th of January, 1924, Ben Pine received a wire from Captain Malloch in Newfoundland saying that *Columbia* had loaded 1,400 barrels of herring and would finish loading in a day or two. She left Bay of Islands on the 16th in company with three other Gloucester vessels and at once ran into a terrible blow. For two days they rode out the storm under nothing but their foresails while the winds continued with unabating fury. Struggling to make any headway at all, *Columbia* at length was able to gain the harbor at Sydney, Nova Scotia, where she put in for shelter until the gales should diminish. For several days she waited there, her companions lying in other Nova Scotian ports. When it appeared to be moderating, she set sail again, only to be greeted once more by a fresh onslaught of near-hurricane winds. Again she was forced to run for shelter, this time coming into Halifax. On Saturday, the 26th, she tried a third time to head for Gloucester and for the third time was nearly overwhelmed by howling gales, which swept the deck with mountainous seas and coated the rigging in freezing spray. On Sunday an enormous wave boarded the vessel and swept Captain Malloch into the stern, severely injuring his leg. With the vessel in dire straits and the skipper in a very painful condition, *Columbia* put about and headed back to Halifax where the captain was landed and taken to a doctor for treatment.

With grim determination, *Columbia* set forth again on Tuesday, now under the command of crewman Capt. Burns Benham. The hurricane winds had abated somewhat and she was able to try once more to head for Gloucester. At long last, after four solid days of beating against heavy head winds and still under

124

foresail for most of the time, she rounded Dog-bar Breakwater and was home. She had been seventeen days coming from Newfoundland. For all the time she had been at sea she was buffeted by the worst weather the winter North Atlantic could offer. At times the wind had reached ninety miles per hour and repeatedly threatened to heave the ship on her beam ends. By the time she docked at the Atlantic Supply Co. wharf, her topsides were completely stripped of paint and her foresail carried a huge rent; her sheets were badly chafed by the constant handling and everywhere were the scars of the awful ordeal.

Upon reaching the wharf she was immediately surrounded by scores of fishermen eager to look at the ship and inquire about the voyage. Happily, all four vessels which had left Bay of Islands together had arrived home safely, with *Columbia* bringing in by far the biggest cargo. She had 1,410 barrels of salt herring in the hold and 140 barrels of pickled herring on deck. How she was able to hold onto the deck cargo nobody could figure out. She had demonstrated a remarkable degree of seaworthiness, but all aboard were critical of the way she steered, both empty and loaded. The blame was placed upon the rake of the mainmast; it was slanted too far aft, they said. As soon as the trip was discharged, the mast was restepped with the mast head being moved forward nearly eighteen inches.

While *Columbia* was gone on her herring voyage, Clayt Morrissey had decided that the time had come to install an engine in the *Henry Ford*. The work was completed early in February.

With spring on the way, *Columbia* was made ready to resume fishing. It took a while to refurbish and prepare the vessel, and it took longer to scare up a crew, but by the 13th of March she was ready to sail on a salt fishing trip in command of Capt. Edwin O. Fudge. She carried stores for a four-month trip but they hoped that with luck she would be back about the middle of June. This time she was going "salt banking," which meant that the fish would be caught on long trawl lines handled by two men in large dories. Another name for the same process was "dory trawling."

125

A standard trawl was a piece of steam-tarred cotton line 300 fathoms long to which were attached, at one fathom intervals, smaller pieces of line each three feet long. On the end of each of these three-foot pieces, or gangings (pronounced ganjings), was a baited fish hook. The trawl line itself, referred to as a ground-line, was fastened at each end to a sixteen-pound anchor. Also fastened to each anchor was a buoy-line which extended up to the buoy, a small numbered wooden keg from which projected a four-foot pole with a little pennant or a black circular marker (black ball). The whole rig—ground-line, ganging, buoys, buoy-lines and anchors—was designated a "trawl." The line part of it was kept in a wooden tub made by sawing a barrel in half. Ergo—"tub-of-trawl."

In preparing to fish, the fishermen baited the trawls aboard the vessel and carefully coiled them into the tubs. Fresh bait, iced or frozen, was used, generally menhaden, herring, mackerel, squid or clams, one piece to a hook. Four to six "tubs-of-trawl" were put into each dory to be carried out in different directions from the schooner. With one man rowing, the other dropped one end of the trawl overboard and paid it out until the end was reached. At this point the next one was bent on and so forth until all had been put out in one long line. Thus the "black ball" or outer extremity of a six-tub set was better than two miles from the vessel. The ground line with its baited hooks lay along the bottom. After an appropriate interval, the line was brought up to the dory where the fish were removed. Sometimes the trawl was brought in and at other times it would be "under-run," meaning it would merely be passed over the dory with the fish being taken off, fresh bait put on the hooks and the line passed back overboard.

A big vessel such as *Columbia* usually carried twelve double or two-man dories. A double dory commonly measured fifteen feet along its bottom and would hold nearly a ton of fish if necessary. On the vessel the fish were dressed and stowed in the same manner used when dory handlining although the fishing was usually done in deeper waters, sometimes to fifty or sixty fathoms. A supply of fresh bait lasted only about ten days, at which point a vessel would have to go in after more. Much of the time on a salt fishing trip was consumed in going back to various ports of the Maritimes for bait. In times when bait was scarce and hard to find, a schooner might spend a week or more going from one port to another looking for a supply. By the time the third or fourth "baiting" was used up the vessel's hold would be full of salted cod and she could start for home.

For once *Columbia* had the good luck she hoped for and was able to start for home by the first of June, having been gone but two and one-half months. She was the first of the spring bankers to arrive back in Gloucester, hailing for 260,000 pounds of salt cod and stocking $9,000. Each man's share was $135. The arithmetic of sharing went like this: The "stock" (in this case $9,000) represented the money paid to the vessel for her fish. One half went to the owners of the vessel and one half went to the crew. The owners, from their half, furnished vessel, dories, trawl gear, salt, bait and stores and paid the skipper his commission, usually seven percent. From their half, the crew paid the cook's wages, usually forty-five or fifty dollars a month, and then shared equally in the remainder. A cook received a share the same as the rest of the crew. The wages were in addition. A cook worked harder than anybody with no relief at all. The manner of division was called the "lay." On a dory handlining trip the lay was different from that of a dory trawler. Here the crew shared half the stock as before, except that each man was paid in proportion to the amount of fish he caught. Thus we had the "highliner" who received the most and the "lowliner" who received the least. If the skipper and the cook had done any fishing, each received one half the money his fish brought plus his regular commission or wage.

It would appear that general public consumption of salt fish was showing a decline by 1924. To bolster sales and promote the business interests of Gloucester, the fishing firms that summer banded together in a co-operative advertising venture which included, among other things, an attractive eight-page booklet containing recipes for cooking "Gloucester Saltfish." One hundred ten thousand copies were printed, with each participating

127

dealer mailing them to his customers. At that time Gloucester was the leading salt fishing port in the country.

Columbia made a second salt banking trip that summer, leaving on June 16, again in command of Captain Fudge. This time she was gone for four and one-half months, returning on October 30. Her trip was a whopper, hailing for 358,000 pounds of salt cod. The stock was $18,781.07, with a share of $360.84. Three firms divided the purchase, paying $5.25 per hundredweight for the fish. One need not be possessed of great mental acuity to see that even with a stock this big, no fisherman ever got rich from his labors, the more especially when it was considered that he worked practically sixteen hours a day, seven days a week, for his modest share. Add to this the fact that he was gone from home for months at a time and was in constant danger for his very life.

With the coming of September, it was once again "that time of year" in Gloucester. It seemed to have reached the point where the approach of fall induced a sort of reflex action among the citizenry prompting them to think and talk racing. Such was now the case. It was September and they were talking about a race between *Columbia* and *Bluenose*. Never mind the fact that the Trustees had announced in Halifax that the trophy would be withdrawn from competition this year because of the unsatisfactory termination of the series last year. Never mind that *Columbia* was far away and would be home no one knew when. The local committee, just to be sure, wired Halifax for confirmation of their announcement. They got it, along with a request to please stop talking about racing. Actually, behind the scenes and among those who really mattered—the contributors—there was little enthusiasm for any race talk this season. Most had had all they wanted of racing last year. The *Boston Traveler* editorialized that a postponement of racing would be a good thing and would give a chance to straighten out rules and procedures. It felt that the races had not been true fishermen's affairs but rather had been taken over and spoiled by wealthy "yachtsmen in their white suits and brass buttons." Nevertheless, Ben Pine said he would be willing to race Angus

Walters in a special match race or races "if a purse could be raised."

Nobody, it appeared, seemed interested to raise one. In their announcement, the Trustees had said, however, that in 1925 Canada would be represented by a boat and crew "prepared to abide by the decisions of the International Committee."

That fall another syndicate was formed in Halifax to build a new Canadian contender.

If *Columbia* was Gloucester's Cinderella who changed back to a scullery maid, it suddenly appeared as if she was about to lose her job as a scullery maid. Nobody seemed to want her anymore. Perhaps it might be more accurate to say that she had suddenly come face to face with the economic facts of life. It was nice to be a Cinderella, but in simple truth it wasn't paying. *Columbia* wasn't paying; she wasn't paying her bills and she wasn't paying her mortgage. She had just discharged a big trip of salt fish, but she hadn't been discharging enough trips like that, and it was salt fish, not racing and headlines and horns and whistles which paid the freight. Actually a combination of circumstances suddenly seemed to converge upon her with the result that she was tied up after the discharge of the big trip in November 1924 and was destined, as it turned out, to stay tied up for nearly seventeen months.

In the first place, times were changing, and along with them Gloucester was changing; its industry was changing, its customers were changing and, more significantly for our story, the vessels were changing. The simple fact was that *Columbia* was an anachronism. Let's face it—she was built to comply with the Deed of Gift and to beat the *Bluenose*. In complying with the Deed of Gift she carried no engine and with no engine it had become almost impossible to gather a crew. She was the last Gloucester vessel built to go fishing without auxiliary power, and fishermen of Gloucester weren't going out any more in all-sail vessels. Clayt Morrissey had recognized this when at length he put an engine in the *Henry Ford*. For better or worse, the fishing industry of Gloucester was never to be the same after that day in 1900 when Capt. Sol Jacobs put to sea in the

129

new *Helen Miller Gould*, the first Gloucester schooner to carry an auxiliary engine.

In the second place, *Columbia*'s bills were not getting paid. A fishing vessel, or any commercial vessel for that matter, was profitable if she worked steadily to earn her keep, but all this racing business had removed considerable segments of time from her earning career and had contributed measurably to her indebtedness. The local race committee had done the best it could to keep abreast of the bills Ben Pine ran up, but there were limits to the generosity of the wealthy donors who had always been counted on to cough up when a racing fund drive was on. From any angle, it cost a lot of money to support racing. Of greater significance, however, was the fact that in the nineteen months of her career, she had made but four fishing trips and one freighting trip. Not enough.

Lastly, there was the matter of financing. A considerable share of the vessel still remained unsold. It appeared that for many investors, *Columbia* had not been an attractive proposition. It had also reached the point where A. D. Story, holder of a ten thousand dollar mortgage on the vessel, wanted his money and was threatening to foreclose.

With the discharge of her latest trip, *Columbia* was stripped of sails, stores and most of her running rigging and taken over to the old Booth salt wharf in East Gloucester and tied up to await further developments. The Associates held their annual meeting on Monday, January 12, 1925, up in the rooms of the Master Mariners' Association and elected Henry F. Brown of Booth Fisheries to be treasurer, replacing Kenneth Ferguson, who resigned for business reasons. Ben Pine was elected president and Marion Cooney clerk. Ben Pine, Capt. William H. Thomas and Capt. Alden Geele were designated the managing committee. What else they did that evening was not revealed.

In April, the *Gloucester Times* ran a photo of a fine new schooner, the *Haligonian*, fresh from a Shelburne, Nova Scotia, shipyard. Built for a group of Halifax businessmen, she was designed by W. J. Roué to beat his *Bluenose*. The picture was shortly followed by an editorial pointing out that Gloucester

130

might very possibly be unable to accept a Canadian challenge to a fishermen's race with no *Columbia* to do it with. It spoke of the fact that she might well have to be sold, and called for a united effort on the part of the general public and of those associations in Gloucester which had the welfare of the city at heart, to save the schooner by purchasing the balance of the stock.

In early May, Treasurer Brown of Columbia Associates presented his case to the Gloucester Chamber of Commerce, asking their help in the matter of financing. At first they agreed to call a mass meeting, but soon had second thoughts, believing that it was more properly a matter for the American Race Committee. It seems that many in the Chamber felt the effort would not be successful and that failure would reflect unfavorably on the Chamber. The race committee considered the question and they too decided to leave it alone. They did say that as individuals they would help *Columbia*'s owners dispose of the stock, some of which, in response to recent publicity, had lately been sold. All of this left the problem right where it began—in the laps of *Columbia*'s owners. Incongruously, the race committee, while turning down aid to their own vessel, began to beat the drums for a fall racing series which, if held, was scheduled to take place off Gloucester.

For reasons of maintenance and preservation *Columbia* was hauled on the railways in late June. Wonder of wonders, they finally discovered what ailed her. She was found to have a split rudder post, which solved then and there the riddle of her steering. A new rudder was made and installed and, with a fresh coat of copper bottom paint, overboard she went and back to her home at the Booth wharf. Perhaps to pay for this and to help stave off the inevitable, Ben Pine and Marion Cooney dipped into their own pockets again, putting $1,100 apiece into the kitty.

On the 30th of September the Columbia Associates held another meeting. It wasn't reported what the financial status of their vessel was at the moment, but the report did say that a decision was made to begin a preliminary fitting of *Columbia* for a race and to place the vessel at the disposal of the American Race Committee for a race at Gloucester or Halifax. The stockholders expressed themselves as "having implicit faith in their schooner" and believed she should have another opportunity to prove herself " the fastest schooner afloat." They went on to say they had heard that no Canadian vessel was willing to come to Gloucester and therefore, "believing that the *Columbia* can beat anything carrying a rudder which flies the flag of our neighborly and friendly province," would be willing to go to Canada. Then, just to show they meant business, they began scraping *Columbia*'s spars.

On the strength of all this, the American Racing Committee met at the Master Mariners' rooms the following Saturday night, October 3, and voted unanimously to send a challenge to Halifax for a race that fall, in Gloucester preferably, but Halifax if not. A week went by with no answer. While they waited, the Associates had *Columbia* hauled out again and spruced up, just in case.

Finally came the reply from Halifax saying that if there were to be races, they would have to be held down there and held between November 5 and November 15. Furthermore, they wanted to combine an elimination race with the main event since there were several eligible Canadian vessels but little enthusiasm for raising money. At this the Americans demurred, saying they wanted no part of a free-for-all nor did they want to wait until so late in the season.

For all practical purposes the reply from Halifax to this closed the door on racing for 1925. They said in effect that it looked too difficult now to raise money for any sort of race and Canadian boats weren't especially interested anyway. Without saying it in so many words they just wished the American committee would stop talking and call it all off.

The Columbia Associates weren't listening. With a new rudder and the vessel all shined up, Ben got a crew to take her out for a spin. They came back beating their breasts and shouting they'd race after all—in a free-for-all or whatever, one vessel or forty-nine. "Just tell us what we can expect for expense money, win or lose." This time the Canadians weren't listening. Neither was

132

A. D. Story; he foreclosed the mortgage. Back went *Columbia* to the old salt wharf.

At 10 A.M. on Saturday, January 16, 1926, *Columbia* went under the hammer. At the time, there were $10,400 in outstanding bills against her, plus A. D. Story's unpaid mortgage of $10,000. Contrary to expectations, autioneer Fred Shackelford received only two bids. The first, for $10,000, was made by a Mr. Edgar S. Taft. Mr. Story then bid $10,100 and the boat was his. As far as the vessel itself was concerned, the only change was to move her from the Booth wharf to Slade Gorton's where she lay until spring.

By late March Ben Pine and Marion Cooney were able to form a new corporation and buy back their *Columbia*. Partners in the new venture with them were Alexander Chisholm of the John Chisholm Fisheries Co. and Miss Ray Adams, Ben's associate in the Atlantic Supply Co. The new corporation took ownership of the vessel and assumed all lien claims. At once they moved her to the Atlantic Supply wharf and began preparations for a dory handline trip. The paper reported that the new owners were influenced in what they had done mainly by public spirit and a desire to keep *Columbia* in Gloucester. It also reported Ben Pine as saying that any stockholder in the old corporation would be welcome in the new.

One cannot but wonder how many of *Columbia*'s old stockholders would have been seriously interested in buying any more shares in the new corporation. With work under way to prepare the ship for a spring fishing trip it was obvious that, for the present at least, no thought was being given to installing an engine in *Columbia*. It would seem that the dismal financial experience of her initial years should have demonstrated beyond any doubt that the time had come when a vessel needed power to be successful. It must be concluded, therefore, and subsequent events appeared to bear this out, that Ben Pine and his new associates were still primarily interested in maintaining *Columbia*'s strict conformance with the terms of the Deed of Gift. Come what may, Ben would have a vessel he could race.

With Capt. John McInnis in command, *Columbia* finally left Gloucester on Tuesday, April 13, bound on a dory handlining trip. Whether somebody left a hatch cover upside down on deck or wore red mittens or said "pig" or what—we don't know, but we do know that on Tuesday, April 27, while running into the harbor of Canso, N. S., to escape a storm, *Columbia* ran ashore and onto some rocks. Maybe it was because she had left on the 13th. She opened up a bad leak which shortly spoiled much of the salt and stores. A tug which happened to be in the vicinity attempted to pull her off without success, so a Canadian cutter was summoned. The cutter managed to free her. The damage seemed not as bad as had been feared at first and temporary measures were taken in Canso to keep her afloat while awaiting a tow to Halifax 130 miles away. By the time she had gotten to Halifax, been hauled on the railways and completed her repairs it was the 13th of May; the repairs alone had taken a week.

The year's fishing season was already well advanced when *Columbia* resumed her voyage, only to find that the fishing was very bad. They found no fish at all on the Grand Banks and poor fishing around St. Mary's. By early July they gave up in disgust and headed home, arriving on Saturday, July 17, with a fare of only 85,000 pounds of salt fish.

Hardly had the trip been discharged when Halifax began to make noises about a possible race in the fall. On July 31 a telegram was received by the American committee telling of Canadian plans to hold an elimination race. It was expected that the winner would come to Gloucester. The wire was quickly followed by a report that entrants to date in the elimination race included the new *Haligonian*, the *Mayotte* and *Bluenose*.

In immediate response, the American committee met to consider the matter. Rightly construing the message to be a challenge, they voted to accept. They felt that the period around October 12 would be a fine time for the series to be held. They further voted to proceed at once with the arrangements and to get *Columbia* ready. One thing more—they voted to organize a campaign for funds. All of this was telegraphed to Mr. Silver of the Trustees, who now answered that Canada would like to race,

134

but most of their boats which had come in with a summer trip wanted to make one more and wouldn't be back in time to have concluded an elimination race by October 12. In any case, he said he would send more word later.

To get into the spirit of the thing, so to speak, Ben Pine accepted a one-day charter for *Columbia*. On August 18 he sailed out of Gloucester with a party of seventy-five ladies and gentlemen, guests of Wetmore Hodges of New York City. They spent the day cruising about Massachusetts Bay. Perhaps as much as anything, the trip served as a try-out for possible racing and as an opportunity to give the canvas a thorough examination. It became apparent that if *Columbia* was going to race, she would need a new suit of sails. Such being the case, a question of eligibility arose, since the Deed of Gift now specified that a vessel's racing sails must have been used in one season's fishing. When apprised of the situation, the Trustees replied that no question of sails would be raised if other requirements were met.

There occurred at this time an event which was to have a very depressing effect on the fishermen of Canada and rendered unlikely any participation by them in a possible race. A terrible storm swept the banks, carrying the schooner *Sylvia Mosher* to her destruction on Sable Island with the loss of twenty-eight men. Missing after the same storm was the schooner *Sadie Knickle*. It had been hoped that the *Sylvia Mosher* would be a contender in the Canadian elimination race. Thus, the plans for this race were cast aside temporarily in respect and sorrow for the lost men.

Into this rather indeterminate dialogue suddenly stepped Clayton Morrissey. On the morning of Wednesday, September 8, he appeared at the office of the Atlantic Supply Co. on Rogers Street and, confronting Ben Pine, announced that, in his opinion, the *Henry Ford* was really a better boat than *Columbia* was, and if Ben was willing, he'd like to demonstrate that premise. In Gloucester, in 1926, that meant but one thing: there was going to be a series that year and a good one.

8 ⋆ *Columbia vs. the Henry Ford*

To a city as anxious to take part in a good racing series as Gloucester was, the news of Captain Morrissey's challenge came like a draught of fresh air. The sad fact of the matter was that the International Series had degenerated into seemingly little more than petty grudge fights closely circumscribed by the regulations and yachtsman's measurements rules of the ubiquitous Deed of Gift. The initial series of 1920 had unquestionably been a good one, but it was now beginning to appear impossible even to arrange a series, what with cross-currents of antagonism and self-interest on the part of both sides. People everywhere were wishing that it might be possible for a number of good fishing vessels to just go out there and race, and never mind a lot of yachting rules. Suddenly, it appeared this wish was about to be granted.

As might be expected, Ben Pine and his new associates at once accepted the challenge. The city was emotionally ripe for an event like this and demonstrated it by the enthusiasm with which it plunged into the preparations. The local committee, actually the American committee for the International Series, met, and at the suggestion of Captains Morrissey and Pine, brought in a few new members who would represent all facets of Gloucester civic and maritime interests. At once plans were made to handle publicity and to hold a splendid banquet while a team of solicitors was delegated to fan out over the city in quest of contributions. It was decided that the race should be open to any "legitimate fishing vessel from any American port."

On Friday of that week Captains Morrissey and Pine got together again and settled on October 2 as the date of their first race. They decided that if there were to be two boats, the series should be a best two out of three; if more, then three out of five. More significantly, they agreed that the racing would be to "fishermen's order" with no hard and fast rules. "Let's see," said

Captain Clayt as they shook hands on the arrangement, "we'd better have a little something to make it interesting. How about $300?—$400?—$500?" "Make it $500," replied Ben. "I guess I can raise that amount."

For the next couple of weeks the preparations went on apace with contributions coming in at a very satisfying rate. The wealthy summer residents of Eastern Point and Bass Rocks were donating generously, as were the business firms throughout the city. Along the waterfront and among the fish firms the spirit was most contagious. The committee decided that a first prize of $1,500 would be offered, with $500 for second. If a third vessel entered, there would be a consolation prize of $100. It was felt that as presently scheduled, the races would conflict with the World Series, so the dates were moved along to Monday, Tuesday and Wednesday, October 11, 12 and 13. An eager member of the committee was Congressman A. Piatt Andrew, who volunteered to see to it that the U. S. Navy supplied some craft to be used as committee and stake boats. In addition to the cash prizes, Frank E. Davis of the fish company and George Fuller of Eastern Point offered to provide two silver trophies. Meanwhile a dispatch from Halifax to a Boston paper indicated that, in view of the dispute of 1923, any further international racing seemed highly unlikely. For his part, Captain Walters was reported to have said that he would talk to Gloucester only after being paid the money taken from him at the last international race and that in any case he was not about to do any racing in American waters. This now, in Gloucester, was of no more than academic interest, although the Gloucester committee, presumably not wishing to appear too provincial in its outlook, did extend its invitation to Canadian vessels to come down if they wished.

As the days prior to race week slipped by, the city once again found itself going all out to prepare for another big event. The committee received an application from the O'Hara Brothers' Boston schooner *Gossoon* and, surprisingly, another from the new *Haligonian* in Halifax. The fund drive was going quite well, with many large contributions noted. The trend of sentiment was indicated by Gloucester's ex-Mayor Davis who said as he made his contribution that he had heretofore never given a nickel, but that this race was to be a "genuine affair." The New York papers wired for accommodations for their reporters while automobile tourists began to converge on Gloucester from all directions to have a look at the racers. Editorial comment in the Boston papers suddenly changed from attitudes of condemnation to expressions of favor and support.

In the evening of Tuesday, September 28, the groups representing the *Ford* and the *Columbia* met with the committee at the rooms of the Master Mariners' Association, where such regulations as there were to be were worked out in a most amicable fashion. All rules regarding ballast, sail area, water line, draft, crew or whatever were swept aside, the only instructions being in matters of passing, rights on a new course, rounding buoys, etc. It was decided that *Columbia* would carry number 3 and *Ford* number 5. Captain Morrissey and Captain Pine each posted his check for $500 with the committee. Captain Morrissey said with a wink that in his opinion the *Henry Ford* right now was superior to anything sailing from an American port in a fishing rig. To this, of course, Ben Pine took immediate exception. As far as the waterfront was concerned, the betting was even money.

The next day both schooners were hauled on the railways to be scrubbed and prettied up, the *Ford* also to have her shaft and propeller removed. All gear and sails were overhauled and a considerable amount of running rigging in both vessels was replaced. *Columbia* needed a new main gaff, the raw stick alone costing $130. It was planned that each would sail plenty of trials to stretch the rigging properly and determine the best disposition of ballast.

In matters Canadian, it was the old story—on again, off again. Having expressed a desire to come to Gloucester, the *Haligonian* now said she couldn't get ready in time. It seems she had stranded and suffered some damage to hull and rigging in the effort to free her, all of which must first be repaired. On second thought, her owners said she might come but the expense of

138

preparation would be more than they could stand. In reply, the Gloucester committee said that since both *Henry Ford* and *Columbia* were each being given $1,000 for expenses, they would do as much for *Haligonian*. In addition the Nova Scotian government itself offered another $1,000. With this they wavered, indicating they might now come—but she needed new sails and that would make the cost really too much. "Name it and you can have it," answered the Gloucester committee, in effect, as Chairman Reed called Halifax on the phone with an offer to lend *Haligonian* a whole suit of sails. Not only that, but he also told Mr. Montague, principal owner of the vessel, that if their boat couldn't get an immediate berth on a railways in Halifax, to bring her to Gloucester and they'd put her on down here. There was more hemming and hawing until finally it was, yes, we'll come but we want a postponement of a couple of weeks. No. A day or two, maybe? No. Scratch *Haligonian*. Scratch *Gossoon*, too, as O'Hara Brothers, in sizing up the competition, evidently decided *Gossoon* to be a little outclassed. Thus as it came down to the wire, it was turning out to be strictly a Gloucester affair, and somehow it seemed that that was what a great many people wanted it to be.

Columbia was first off the ways, followed in a couple of days by the *Ford*. Both skippers immediately set about tuning their vessels and making practice runs off Cape Ann, and both, on returning to the harbor, tied up side by side at the Atlantic Supply Co. wharf. Each skipper was accompanied on his trial spins by his own coterie of expert mariners. On the *Columbia* Ben had Commodore Roy Pigeon of the Cottage Park Yacht Club for an adviser and Capt. Norman Ross as mate. Sailmaker and partner Marion Cooney was along to keep an eye on his canvas. On the *Ford*, Clayt had Jack Mehlman, reputed to be one of the cleverest yacht handlers of the North Shore, as his adviser. Each skipper was able to get in four good days of sailing prior to racing, and each, while taking good opportunity to test and try his vessel, made the trips a pleasant holiday for all on board. There were many invited guests, ladies and gentlemen, out for the ride, as well as cameramen and reporters. They experienced some thrilling sailing, too, for the wind blew at better than twenty knots on a couple of trial days, and there were times when *Columbia* was rolled down to her sheer poles as she boiled along from Thatcher's to Half-way Rock. She was sporting a whole new set of headsails as well as a new foresail. She was having a little trouble, however, with some of the new running rigging, and on Sunday, the day before the first race, her fore gaff topsail somehow became caught and ripped in two, but there was plenty of time to fix it. The foresail on the *Henry Ford* was the old one borrowed from *Columbia* for this occasion. Ben was taking a lot of pains with *Columbia*'s ballast and kept a pile of sand bags on the wharf with which to make any needed adjustments. She was carrying about 110 tons, which still left her a little over her designed line. All in all, the whole affair was enveloped in a fine and festive atmosphere of friendliness and cooperation, with a relaxed "let's have a good time" feeling in both boats. And why not? Nobody had anything to lose. Considering the prizes announced by the committee, both vessels would probably come out a little ahead financially whether they won or lost.

The committee had been doing its job well and had decided on Saturday that first prize would be $1,750 and second $1,250. Each vessel was to receive $1,000 in addition for expenses. Congressman Andrew had also done his job well, securing two Coast Guard cutters for stake boats and two destroyers, one for the committee and one for the press. The "Frank E. Davis Trophy" had been instituted as an award for the "fastest sailing fishing schooner in the North Atlantic" and was expected to be in yearly competition. Any vessel winning it three times would, however, retain permanent possession. The Fuller Cup was to be awarded only for this series and was given merely as a gesture of goodwill and affection for Gloucester by George Fuller of Worcester and Eastern Point, who, by the way, had been made a crewman on *Columbia*.

Monday, October 11, was the first race day. It happened also to be the seventy-second birthday of Arthur D. Story, who was about to enjoy the singular pleasure of watching two of his own creations as they engaged each other in competition. To avoid any possibility of conflict in departure, *Henry Ford* had tied up the night before at Davis Bros. wharf and was away by 8:30, leaving the harbor without assistance. *Columbia* left from her Atlantic Supply wharf about nine o'clock and, after a short assist from a small dragger, lost no time in setting sail and making for the breakwater. By 9:30 both vessels were outside Eastern Point and testing the air and securing all rigging while they waited for the ten o'clock starting gun.

It was planned to use the same course as that used in the International Series of 1922. If the moderate northwest wind at starting time continued, it meant a five mile close reach from the starting line to the first mark off Milk Island. From there it became another reach for ten miles back down the bay to the second mark off Magnolia; thence a run offshore to the outer or third mark; thence a beat of ten miles back to Milk Island and the last five miles a beat to the finish. As it turned out, the wind backed to the westerly about noon and the fourth leg became another close reach instead of a beat, making for windward work only in the last five miles to the finish.

As the two boats approached the start, the *Columbia* found herself in the windward position and, with rails under, shot down for the line. The *Ford* had taken a little too long to jibe, and though she crossed the line fifty yards ahead of *Columbia* was almost immediately passed as *Columbia* rushed by on a port tack. The *Ford* was slightly blanketed but soon recovered and hung on close astern of *Columbia*, trailing by 31 seconds at the first mark. Here the *Ford* again had trouble jibing and lost a few more seconds, but again she was able to pull up to *Columbia*, although never quite able to pass. The winds were not at all strong and whenever it breezed up *Columbia* would move ahead, only to have the *Ford* come along as it eased off. At one point along this leg *Columbia* found herself in trouble with her staysail, almost allowing the *Ford* to squeeze by, but Ben got it straightened out and continued to hold his position. Once more they jibed as they reached the second mark, with *Columbia* in the lead now by 41 seconds.

The next leg was the ten mile run off shore and here the *Ford* finally caught up with *Columbia*, passing her to windward. Immediately, Ben commenced a luffing match which carried the boats some three miles to the eastward of the course. At length Captain Morrissey jibed, only to be followed by *Columbia*, and now they worked themselves three miles off on the other side with *Ford* keeping a comfortable lead. The further off shore they went, the weaker grew the wind, so that as they approached the third mark, there was little more than steerage way. This time the *Ford* rounded the buoy with a 40 second lead.

As they headed back on the reach to Milk Island, *Henry Ford* seemed to be holding her own and in no danger, when suddenly *Columbia* acquired a mysterious burst of speed which brought her up and through the *Ford's* weather. Taking the lead she held it for the balance of the leg, although both vessels overstood the mark. *Columbia* had now regained a 38 second lead. With the final five miles a dead beat, *Columbia* at once showed a superiority in windward work. Steadily increasing her margin, she crossed the line the winner by 1 minute and 4 seconds.

	Columbia	Henry Ford
Start	10:00:00	10:00:00
1st mark	10:23:15	10:23:46
2nd mark	11:11:44	11:12:25
3rd mark	1:01:00	1:00:00
4th mark	2:13:05	2:13:43
Finish	2:49:56	2:51:00

Actually the race was so close as to be in doubt until the rounding of the fourth mark, with *Columbia* really winning in the last six miles. The race had been largely a battle of skippers and at the finish it was Ben Pine's day. Old fishermen of the waterfront marveled at the way he had done it. One was heard to comment, "Piney sure outfoxed Clayt!" and from another, "It beats me how Piney learned to sail. Clayt's been handling vessels all his life and Piney ain't even a fisherman!" In any case, it seemed to be agreed that although there hadn't been much wind, it had been one of the most exciting races ever sailed in Massachusetts Bay.

After Monday's close race and with the next day a holiday, the "back shore" of Cape Ann was black with people to watch the next contest. Afloat were a dozen or more fishing draggers loaded to the gunwales with happy holiday crowds ready to follow the schooners around the course. The weather was fair and wind conditions were virtually a duplicate of the day before, except it held true from the northwest all day. This meant that the course would be the same but the leg back to Milk Island from off shore would be a thresh to windward instead of a reach.

The *Ford* was first over the line and not to be "outfoxed" again. Clayt easily led *Columbia* on the reach to the first mark. With sheets broad off he gained considerably on his rival, reaching the first mark with a margin of 1 minute 14 seconds. Here he again had trouble in jibing around the buoy and lost some time, but was able to recover quickly and took the honors in the luffing match along the second leg. In spite of this Ben Pine was able to bring *Columbia* up and with skillful maneuvering actually rounded the second mark 12 seconds ahead of *Henry Ford*. From here on it was *Columbia*'s race all the way. The wind picked up a little, and as they went into the fourth leg *Columbia* left no doubt in anyone's mind that she was the better boat to windward as she increasingly outdistanced the *Ford*. At the last mark before the finish she was leading by 5 minutes and 28 seconds. At this point we quote William U. Swan, reporter for the *Boston Evening Transcript*:

"In the last leg from Milk Island to the finish, the *Columbia* was held in to the beach and dropped a half minute of her lead by her wide course, but she was a grand sight as she came tearing down from Bass Rocks to the whistler with scuppers boiling, her crew cheering and all hands yelling and whistling, while her reception as she rounded the breakwater and ran up the harbor is a thrilling remembrance to thousands. One by one her sails were doused, the mainsail coming down as she rounded the end of the dock, and under bare poles she drifted practically into the waiting arms of the craziest crowd Gloucester has seen in many a day." In short, *Columbia* had won the race, the series and the trophies.

	Columbia	*Henry Ford*
Start	10:00:20	10:00:10
1st mark	10:26:15	10:25:01
2nd mark	11:47:11	11:47:23
3rd mark	2:04:48	2:08:19
4th mark	2:59:29	3:04:57
Finish	3:34:18	3:39:06

In short order, *Columbia* was joined at the wharf by Captain Clayt and the *Henry Ford*, the crews of both vessels immediately engaging in a "jollification" to gladden the heart. With Ben Pine as the genial host, the whole crowd became one happy family, and, winner or loser, a good time was had by all. At length "Rear Admiral" Nate MacLeod of the *Columbia* organized the tumultuous crews and, headed by the Gloucester Cadet Band, which had already been playing all day aboard the excursion dragger *Herbert Parker*, a parade was started up through the city. Captain Pine and Captain Morrissey proudly marched side by side accompanied by Capt. Norman Ross, mainsheet man of the *Columbia*, and Capt. Elroy Prior, his counterpart on the *Ford*. For two hours the parade and celebration continued, with the crews eventually winding up in a number of trucks and autos on their way to the Bass Rocks estate of George Fuller, where the celebration finally ran out of steam.

Wednesday evening was the occasion of the banquet and "to-do" at the Gloucester City Hall. The skippers and crews met at the rooms of the Master Mariners' Association in Post Office Square and, again preceded by the Gloucester Cadet Band, marched to the City Hall Auditorium. Separating at the door, *Columbia*'s crew marched down the aisle at the right side of the hall and the *Henry Ford*'s crew down the left, amid tumultuous applause.

A splendid banquet was enjoyed, after which committee chairman and toastmaster William MacInnis arose to express the thanks of the committee to all who had contributed to the success of the series. He then introduced each crewman and each skipper. (Loud applause for each.) Now, at a signal, Major Owen Steele and fellow officers of the High School R.O.T.C.

came to the stage bearing the Frank E. Davis Trophy, which ex-Mayor Davis himself presented to Captain Pine. (Rousing cheers.) Mr. George Fuller was then called upon to do the honors for the Fuller Cup. He began by making a very gracious statement of his pleasure and privilege at knowing such splendid men as the crews and skippers of the two vessels. As he was speaking, other officers of the R.O.T.C. appeared with the Fuller Cup, at which Mr. Fuller remarked that he had recently "been hearing a lot about splitting prizes and purses, and if any splitting is to be done, I'm going to do it!" With this, he produced a great sheaf of greenbacks, remarking that he thought it wise to put less into cups and more into the hands of the captains. So saying, he divided the bundle of bills, stuffing part into the cup and the rest into the hands of Captain Morrissey. (Cheers.) Then, noting that since he had himself been a member of *Columbia*'s crew, he felt someone else should make the presentation of the cup, and, turning to Captain Morrissey, asked him to do it. The captain seemed pleased to oblige, and, taking the cup, passed it to Ben Pine with a most hearty handshake. (Tumultuous cheers.)

Mr. Fuller, however, wasn't yet finished. Continuing to speak, he produced a large silver bowl which he placed on the table before him, saying as he did so that there ought to be something in silver for the loser as well as the winner.

"I've been to a physician to fill this bowl," he said, "and although I've had much trouble, I think I've succeeded. I told the doctor that I sailed on the *Ford* against the *Bluenose* and had never been the same since." (Laughter.) "'Any man who has done that certainly needs a stimulant,' said the Doc." (More laughter.)

At this Mr. Fuller again reached under the table and produced a large old pewter pitcher. Carefully placing a lining in the silver bowl, he poured out 250 silver dollars, all of which, bowl and cartwheels, he presented to Captain Morrissey. (Storm of cheering and applause.) As he resumed his seat, the band struck up a stirring march and everybody cheered for everybody else. It could be heard way down the street.

In conclusion, chairman MacInnis presented each skipper his

prize and expense money, receiving, in turn, gracious remarks of appreciation and tribute from both. Each crewman was presented a safety razor kit from the Fairbanks Morse Co., after which the crews marched from the hall to yet another and final round of tumultuous applause. By now anybody left in the hall was limp. All who had been in attendance agreed that it was difficult to recall any public gathering in Gloucester in recent years equal to this one for sheer enthusiasm and good feeling.

All rumors, reports and protestations to the contrary notwithstanding, the Canadians were indeed thinking about racing, and were thinking enough about it to be proceeding with an elimination series planned for the very weekend following the Gloucester races. The American committee knew about it and felt that a challenge would probably come to the winner of the Gloucester series, although there was a decided lack of enthusiasm around Gloucester for any further contests that year. Ben Pine was well aware of it too and had taken pains to announce that if an international series was to be held, and if *Columbia* was the American entrant, Clayton Morrissey would be her skipper. Immediately after Tuesday's race, Ben wired a challenge to Halifax for a race with the Canadian winner. As a matter of fact, he and Captain Morrissey decided to go to Nova Scotia and see the races for themselves, taking the Friday afternoon train for Halifax.

The first race was held on Saturday in a spanking twenty-five knot breeze. *Bluenose* was the easy winner with second place *Haligonian* coming in about 15 minutes later. It was plain to see that the Bluenose victory was due in large measure to the experience of Angus Walters and his crew. The second race on Monday found the vessels unable to complete the course in time, although *Bluenose* was leading by nearly two miles when the race was called off. That night Captain Walters said that since his *Bluenose* had clearly demonstrated her superiority he should be allowed to take the prize and go home. He further said that if he were compelled to sail another race, he would have nothing to do with an international race, off Halifax or anywhere else.

146

The next morning the other vessels—and *Bluenose*—appeared at the starting line. Once more the winds died and the race could not be completed. Once more *Bluenose* was ahead at the finish, this time by 22 minutes. Once more Angus threatened to go home.

On Wednesday, with the time limit raised from five to six hours, the contestants sailed again for the fourth time. A situation arose near the start in which *Haligonian* hailed *Bluenose* for sea room. The call went unheeded and *Haligonian's* bobstay struck the *Bluenose*. The *Haligonian* was stopped dead in her tracks as *Bluenose* crowded the buoy to take the lead, going on to win the race by a 6 minute margin in the time of 4 hours, 23 minutes. Ben Pine and Clayton Morrissey were grateful that for once the ensuing rhubarb was strictly a Canadian family affair. Both men came back to Gloucester feeling that the Canadian series had been very disappointing. Nothing official was heard from Halifax regarding Ben's challenge, although rumor had it that Angus wanted to challenge *Columbia* for a series to be sailed off Boston. In reply to a reporter's question, Ben was most emphatic in saying that it would be Gloucester or nothing. And "nothing" it was as *Columbia* began preparations for a herring voyage to Newfoundland and *Bluenose* was stripped in preparation for winter lay-up at Lunenburg.

9 ★ The End

For the first time since the 19th of July, *Columbia* was once
again a work boat as she sailed from Gloucester Harbor on Monday, November 1, bound for Bay of Islands, Newfoundland, on
a herring voyage. Her commander was now Capt. Matthew
Critchett, himself a Newfoundlander. It took her nearly two
weeks to make the trip, and it was not until the 17th that any
word was received of her arrival. The herring fishing was very
poor in Newfoundland that season and all the American boats
there were finding it difficult to purchase a cargo. To expedite
matters, Ben Pine himself went to Newfoundland shortly after
Columbia got there and remained for about three weeks looking after *Columbia*'s interests. He found the season to be the
poorest it had been in years. The schooners *Louise R. Sylva* and
Thomas S. Gorton transferred what fish they had to the *Geor-
gianna* in order that she might have a full load and start for
home. It was the 30th of December before *Columbia* was loaded
and able to leave.

She sailed in company with the *Thomas S. Gorton*, Capt.
Wallace Parsons, the two vessels leaving together from the harbor at Bay of Islands. True to the traditions of sailing fishermen,
both skippers sensed the possibilities here for a race and at
once set all the sail they dared, crowding their vessels to the
limit as they had headed for home. In marked contrast to the
voyage to Newfoundland, *Columbia* arrived home in four days
—just four hours *behind* the *Gorton*. She had brought in 1,400
barrels of salt herring.

Columbia remained in Gloucester for two weeks and sailed
January 17, 1927, on a second herring voyage, again in command
of Captain Critchett. In recognition of the poor season the Canadian Fisheries Board extended the Newfoundland herring
fishing season from January 31 to February 15. Since the fishing

148

suddenly seemed to improve and the weather was suitable for curing, *Columbia* was able to get a cargo much more quickly this time and left Belleoram, Newfoundland, on Saturday, February 26, with a cargo of 1,450 barrels of salt and frozen herring. It was the 12th of March when she got back to Gloucester.

While *Columbia* had been away on her latest trip, the annual Sportsmen's Show had been held at Mechanics Building in Boston. A feature of the show which attracted much attention was a splendid rigged model of *Columbia* made by Bernard B. Bancroft of Salem. A few weeks later Mr. Bancroft came to Gloucester and presented his model to Ben Pine, who placed it in the window of the Atlantic Supply Co. It remained there for several years.

With spring close at hand it was once again time to prepare *Columbia* for the season's dory handlining trips. She was made ready and sailed for the Grand Banks on Thursday, April 14, the first salt fisherman to leave Gloucester that spring. Her captain now was Lewis Wharton of Liverpool, Nova Scotia. The fishing was good and the trip was uneventful. They returned on the 27th of June with a fare of 350,000 pounds of salt cod, which was sold to the Gorton-Pew Fisheries Co. After a day or two of rest, the stores were replenished and on July 3rd *Columbia*, with Captain Wharton, sailed on her second handlining trip of the season.

Though gone but twelve days, she put into the Captain's home town of Liverpool, Nova Scotia, on July 15, evidently for more stores, leaving on the same day. On the morning of August 23 the Gloucester schooner *Herbert Parker*, Capt. John Carrancho, sighted *Columbia* lying at anchor some fifty miles or so north of Cape Sable, and sailed alongside to speak with Captain Wharton, who told Captain Carrancho that the fishing this trip had so far been very poor and that he had very little fish below decks. After visiting for a bit, Captain Carrancho sailed the *Parker* off to the westward. Along towards night, after parting company with a big Portuguese three-master whose skipper was a friend of his, Captain Carrancho sailed back to where *Columbia* had been, but found she had weighed anchor and gone.

A torrential downpour enveloped Cape Ann on the afternoon

of Wednesday, August 24. The leading story in the *Gloucester Times* the next day described the storm and noted that while the rains about Gloucester had been heavy with little wind, there had been no real damage, a circumstance in marked contrast to other regions in central and southeastern Massachusetts, where storm damage had been very heavy. It went on to say that New England on the whole had been fortunate as a terrific hurricane had passed by some distance out to sea with consequent damage to shipping and especially to the fishing fleets.

How extensive the damage was became apparent when reports came in on Friday of the great destruction of property and ships in Nova Scotia. An unknown number of vessels had been driven ashore and wrecked, with reports that some were from Gloucester. On Saturday, vessels which had survived the storm began to arrive in port with stories of their experiences in the terrible gale. Each brought tales of death and disaster among the fishing fleets. By Monday some American vessels which had experienced the storm were arriving at the Boston Fish Pier bearing the scars of their own encounters. One of these was the *Mayflower*, whose skipper, Capt. Alvaro Quadros of Gloucester, had been swept overboard to his death. In the awful uproar of that terrible night, no one had seen him go or could tell how he was lost.

On Tuesday one of Gloucester's own, the *Edith C. Rose*, limped into the harbor bearing dreadful tales of her experiences in the hurricane. The crew told how there had been no time to do anything to secure ship, so quickly had the awful gale come upon them. It had become a matter of every man for himself. In no time, seemingly, the vessel was hove down on her beam ends until the crosstrees were almost in the water, with the hull buried by a succession of mountainous seas. They frankly confessed that many had cried in fear. After what seemed an eternity, the vessel, as if alive, shook herself free and righted herself, although by then she was nearly in a sinking condition. The crew were forced to bail the cabin and forecastle with buckets to save the ship. Everything movable on deck was swept away, even the little gasoline hoisting machine.

The next day the men of the *Marion McLoon* came home with their own tales of a most harrowing experience. A little schooner, one of those managed by Ben Pine, the *McLoon* had been driven onto the rocks near Whitehead, Nova Scotia the crew being forced to take to the rigging to save themselves. For hours they had clung there until wind and waves abated enough for them to wade ashore.

On Thursday none other than the *Bluenose* arrived in Lunenburg in a damaged condition. Her anchor was gone, most of her hawser, all of the loose gear on deck, and every sail was ripped. She had been fishing on Mizzen Banks when the storm hit. Said Captain Walters, "There was no canvas ever made to stand such a gale. In all my seagoing experience I've never seen the barometer go down and come up as quick as it did on that occasion."

The hurricane and its effects notwithstanding, the American Race Committee met in the rooms of the Master Mariners' Association on Wednesday night, September 7. Present were about twenty-five men, including Captains Pine and Morrissey. They talked about plans for a Gloucester elimination race the following month. At Ben Pine's suggestion, the committee voted to notify the Canadian committee that the winner of the Gloucester race would like to race with *Bluenose* or another Canadian boat, at either Gloucester or Halifax. As they thought about this, they decided it would be better to send a telegram expressing merely a desire to resume the International Series. Ben, however, said that if *Columbia* won the Gloucester race, she would sail to Halifax with Clayt Morrissey at the wheel and the flags of both countries at her peak and say when she got there: "Here we are, come and race us!" "We'll go down and wait ten days," he said, "and we'll race for money, cup or nothing. Then we'll have made them 'put up or shut up'!" In other words, he didn't like the rumors he'd been hearing from Canada that Gloucester didn't want to race. Before adjourning, the committee tentatively set the dates of October 11, 12 and 13 for the local elimination race.

On Friday, reports were received expressing grave fears for

the fate of two Lunenburg schooners, the *Clayton Walters* and the *Joyce Smith*. Nothing had been heard from either since the hurricane. It was felt in Gloucester that this would put a damper on any plans for racing in the coming season. That weekend somebody was reported to have found a dory on Sable Island marked *Columbia*.

In an interview with a man from the *Gloucester Times* the following Wednesday, Ben Pine said that in his opinion the dory found on the island was not one carried by the vessel. He told how the *Herbert Parker* had spoken the *Columbia* on the day before the storm and that she had been fishing the western edge of Western Bank. He felt she could not possibly have gotten in a position off Sable Island before the storm hit. He went on to say that about sixty of *Columbia's* old dories had been sold to different schooners and that in all probability the dory found on the island was one of these; also, that *Columbia* was not expected home until the first of October, and, equipped with brand new canvas as she was, Ben thought she could have made port if the occasion demanded.

The following Saturday a number of Nova Scotia captains got together and decided to go out to Sable Island as a group in an attempt to identify some of the new wrecks cast up there. In the course of their discussions, the question was raised concerning the installation of radios aboard the vessels of their fleet. Several felt that if there had been radios on the schooners, much of the recent loss could have been avoided. Others, however, said that while radios might be a good thing, many owners didn't install them because the government did not broadcast storm warnings.

It was with a sigh of relief that Gloucesterites picked up their *Gloucester Daily Times* on Monday, September 19. In banner headlines it said, "*Columbia* Safe After Storm." The story told how Capt. Lemuel Spinney had informed Ben Pine that his schooner, the *Oretha F. Spinney*, had sighted *Columbia* while bound in from a halibuting trip last week. The vessels had passed on Quero. He said he didn't speak her but knew it was *Columbia*. He hadn't spoken her because, as he said, he wasn't aware that there was any anxiety concerning the vessel. As a matter of fact, he knew nothing of the great storm, having himself been on the Grand Banks. He hoped, however, that his report would quiet the ugly rumors of the past two weeks. That same weekend five Lunenburg skippers went to Sable Island to look at the wrecks. They reported that nothing among the debris they had seen was in any way recognizable to them.

On Tuesday, September 20, the Halifax office of the Marine and Fisheries Department put out the following bulletin:

"Anxiety regarding the safety of the Gloucester fishing schooner and noted racer, *Columbia*, which has been expressed in many quarters since the storm of August 24, was definitely removed yesterday (September 19) when the local office announced that *Columbia* had reported herself as fishing on Quero on September 7." In Gloucester they were puzzled by the report. Did it refer to Captain Spinney's statement or had *Columbia* definitely spoken another vessel? Reports or no reports, people were definitely uneasy about *Columbia*—more so than anyone wanted to admit. And they were growing more uneasy in Gloucester day by day.

On the 24th of September the Nova Scotia papers announced that another Canadian schooner, the big *Uda R. Corkum* of Lunenburg, was officially declared lost in the August hurricane. This brought the Canadian total of known losses to four vessels with the deaths now of eighty men. The storm disaster was described as the worst in the history of the Nova Scotia fleet.

By the 1st of October, Gloucester's concern and anxiety for her *Columbia* broke into the open as the *Gloucester Times* in the headline for the day proclaimed: "Fear Fate of Schooner *Columbia*—Cutter Tampa ordered to Sable Island to search for racer." The paper went on to catalog all of the signs and omens of disaster which it had obviously heretofore been reluctant to print. It cited first the fact that actually no positive word had been received from *Columbia* since the day of the storm; it spoke of the fact that *Columbia* had now been gone since July 3rd and remembered, too, that almost every man aboard including Captain Wharton was a Nova Scotian. The piece concluded with a description of Captain Carrancho's visit with Captain Wharton.

It seems that on the day after the storm a pair of oars marked *Columbia* had floated up on Sable Island. This was not taken seriously since it was reported no other wreckage there was identified with the ship; but then came the report of finding some "Gold Medal" flour bags and some "New Jersey" brand milk cans, neither of which was carried by Canadian vessels. Some days later the Canadian cutter *Arras* found some oak hatch covers floating at sea. Canadian vessels didn't have oak hatch covers.

In spite of an outward confidence that *Columbia* was all right, it was Ben Pine who asked to have the *Tampa* sent to look for her. In commenting upon this he said, "She has grub enough for four months and we didn't expect her back until along about the fifth of this month (October). When Wharton left here and asked me when we wanted the vessel back, I told him to stay until he had a trip, and that the race, if there was to be one, should not be considered. We have heard so much talk about wreckage being found on the island that we thought it only right to send a patrol boat down to look for it. We never intended anyone should know that the *Tampa* was going, but now that it's out, all I can say is that I still think the *Columbia* is all right."

On the day of the *Times* story the *Halifax Chronicle* carried a report that the schooner *Frances G. Roué* had arrived in Halifax two days earlier bearing a dory plank with the name *Columbia* stenciled on it in yellowish paint. The piece of wood was about five feet long and a five fathom line was attached to it. The remnant had been found about sixty miles to the west southwest of the northeast light on Sable Island. The same schooner had sighted a vessel's main boom floating in the sea. The boom was shirred for a riding sail.

The cutter *Tampa* left Boston on Saturday, October 1, with Capts. Edward Proctor, John Farrell and Nathan McLeod aboard as guides and observers. They were gone a week, during which time the cutter crossed and recrossed the banks under conditions of good visibility. She cruised the length of the grounds from Emerald Bank to Quero. They found no floating wreckage themselves nor did they encounter a vessel which had seen any. The captains went ashore on Sable Island and interviewed the men of the life saving station. These men had found one pair of oars marked *Columbia*, six pairs of American-style ash oars having no marks, and the pieces of *two* dories, one marked *Columbia* and the other bearing the letters *Col*. It developed that the U.S. Coast Guard cutter *Jackson* had also been cruising about searching for evidence and had called at the island. In fifteen days she had found nothing more than the men of the *Tampa* did. It was a discouraged trio of Gloucester captains who came ashore from the *Tampa* the following Saturday. Still Ben Pine would not be convinced.

On Monday, October 19, Capt. Iver Carlson of the *Acushla* arrived at Boston Fish Pier from a halibuting trip. He reported sighting what must have been the same main boom seen by the *Frances Roué* which he identified as coming from a dory handliner. He said it was shirred for a riding sail.

In the *Gloucester Times* of October 18 Captain Pine published an open letter to the U. S. Coast Guard in which he thanked the men of the *Tampa* and all others concerned for the splendid effort made in the search for *Columbia*. He further thanked Mr. W. W. Lufkin for arranging the use of the *Tampa*. Ben's confidence was waning at last.

On Wednesday, October 26, a whole dory bearing the name *Columbia* was brought in to the Boston Fish Pier by the Gloucester haddocker *Mary Sears*. Designated #11, it contained a bait knife with the letter M carved on the handle and a length of buoy line. The dory plug was not in its proper place but was tied to the inside of the boat. The bottom of the dory was badly fouled, indicating that it had been floating a long time. The *Sears* had found it about sixty miles southeast of Liverpool, Nova Scotia. As he looked at the dory Captain Pine finally believed that his beloved *Columbia* was gone. The *Gloucester*

155

Times of Saturday, October 29, at long last sadly bore the head-lines: "No Hope Now for *Columbia*—Lost with all hands in the gale of August 24 off Sable Island." It was over.

Inevitably it seems to be human nature after an experience of this kind to attempt to figure out what happened and why or how. As soon as it had been decided once and for all that *Columbia* was gone, interested people began to reconstruct the situation by putting together what fragments of information were available. Bits of news about the vessel continued to come in for some time. For example, it developed that on the same day she had been spoken by Captain Carrancho of the *Herbert Parker*, she also was seen by the Lunenburg schooner *R. H. McKenzie*. Of greater significance was the story of Capt. Angus Tanner of the *Margaret B. Tanner*. He told how his vessel and four others were anchored in a little bight off Sable Island on the day of the storm. It was a dead calm at the time. As they rode there a sudden little puff struck the group of vessels. Sens-ing danger, Captain Tanner at once made sail and got out. He later limped into Shelburne with most of his top hamper gone and only a stub of a mainmast. Three of the vessels he left behind were the *Uda R. Corkum*, the *Joyce Smith* and *Columbia*. All went to their doom. Thus it would appear that Captain Tanner was the last man to have seen *Columbia*.

Although the five Lunenburg captains who had gone out to Sable to view the wreckage cast up there had not been able to identify positively anything they had seen, some one else had gone there a little later and pronounced that some of the wreck-age was definitely that of the *Uda R. Corkum*. This same indi-vidual apparently was unable to recognize any of the other debris.

Then there was the dory brought in by the *Mary Sears*. In the first place the plug was not in; then the painter had been cut off short at the bow with a knife, all of which would indi-cate somebody was in an awful hurry to use it. From all of these bits and pieces came a consensus of opinion that, as so often happened on the banks in a group of vessels, *Columbia* had been lost through violent collision with one or more of the other

156

vessels. But then again, it was still quite as likely that she had managed to get out only to be hove down beyond recovery or even capsized. No one would ever really know.

It was almost prophetic, in a way, that the last port visited by *Columbia* was Captain Wharton's own home town. A photograph was taken of *Columbia* as she left port that day, in which the crew happily lined the rail for the photographer. The captain was very fond of his home and family and had long made a practice of writing every day to his wife and daughter. Whenever the opportunity presented itself, he would deliver a packet of letters to a passing vessel with the request that they be posted when the vessel reached shore. Usually such a chance would come along about every two weeks, but by early October it had been six weeks since Mrs. Wharton had last heard from her husband.

To that long, long roll of mariners who had sailed from Gloucester, never to return, were added these following twenty-two names:

Lewis Wharton, Master, married, age 57	Liverpool, N. S.
Rupert Bragg, cook, married, age 46	Dorchester, Mass.
Isaac Gould, married, age 60	Gloucester, Mass.
Colin Hawley, married, age 30	Gloucester, Mass.
William Colp	Bucksport, Maine
Leo White	Bucksport, Maine
Arthur Firth, married, age 60	Shelburne, N. S.
James MacAloney, single, age 34	Parrsboro, N. S.
James McLeod, married, age 63	Liverpool, N. S.
Foster McKay, single, age 20	West Green Harbor, N. S.
Clayton Johnson, age 26	West Green Harbor, N. S.
Carroll Williams, married, age 28	West Green Harbor, N. S.
Enos Belong, married, age 54	West Green Harbor, N. S.
Joseph Mayo, age 54	Halifax, N. S.
Thomas Hayden, age 39	Shelburne, N. S.
Frank Dedrick, age 52	Shelburne, N. S.
Allison Firth, cachee, single, age 17	Shelburne, N. S.
George Williams, age 56	Liverpool, N. S.
Robert Stewart, married	Liverpool, N. S.
George H. Mayo, age 28	Halifax, N. S.
Samuel Belong, single	Green Harbor, N. S.
Charles L. Huskins, single, age 20	Green Harbor, N. S.

On the very day that the loss of *Columbia* was announced came the news that another of Gloucester's vessels had gone down. In a circumstance wholly unrelated to the great storm, the schooner *Avalon* was struck by an Italian liner on October 29 while off Cape Race and sent to the bottom with the loss of eleven more men. Gloucester felt it had been dealt some heavy blows and the response it made to the relief of the bereaved was indeed a tribute to the spirit of the city.

Immediately upon news of the latest disaster, the American Race Committee sprang into action in a cause whose motive this time was purely human charity. A fund drive was instituted to raise $20,000 to aid the anguished families of the lost crewmen, of both *Columbia* and the *Avalon*. As a starter, Clayt Morrissey, Ben Pine and each of the other *Columbia* associates gave $100. They were quickly followed by citizens and agencies in every segment of city life. The business firms made donations, as did the people of Eastern Point, many very generously. In six weeks' time when the drive was finished, it had been oversubscribed by $3,000.

So at last we reach the end of this narrative. Crowded into the fifty-two months of *Columbia*'s lifetime had been the whole gamut of experience to which a ship could be subject. The creature of a remarkable era, she had been born as a result of controversy, she found herself involved in controversy and even her violent death had been controversial. She had sailed quiet seas at work and at play and had been buffeted by the worst the North Atlantic could offer; a stinking salt fisherman one day, she could be transformed into a white-winged creature of beauty the next. Her forecastle had been home to a great many men for long periods of time and she had known many hands at her helm; she had experienced collisions, groundings, litigation, triumphs and defeat. Her troubles essentially stemmed from the fact that it was impossible for a schooner to be a racing machine and a profitable fishing vessel at one and the same time. It was as a fishing vessel, however, that *Columbia* perhaps left her important mark. Although the Gloucester waterfront didn't realize it at the time, *Columbia*, as she sailed on July 3, 1927, was the last salt fishing vessel to sail from the port. *Columbia* had gone, and with her had gone one of the most distinctive phases of Gloucester's famous industry.

Epilogue

During the forenoon of Tuesday, January 3, 1928, the large Canadian steam trawler *Venosta* arrived back in her home port of Halifax. She was a big steel vessel, some 330 gross tons and about 145 feet long, owned by the National Fish Co. of Halifax. The *Venosta* had been dragging on the grounds off Sable Island and her trip had been cut short by the loss of about six hundred dollars' worth of her trawl gear which had become fouled as they attempted to haul it back. How that gear became fouled is one of the most weird and dramatic episodes ever to unfold in the annals of the sea.

The *Venosta* had been working the grounds about forty miles to the west southwest of Sable Island or, expressed a little differently, about 115 miles to the south-southeast of Halifax, when it happened. The time was shortly before 2:00 A.M. on the morning of Sunday, January 1. With a pale and misty moon dimly illuminating her path across the black wastes of the Atlantic, the big trawler was steaming slowly along dragging her nets along the bottom, sweeping up everything in her way. Suddenly, with a lurch and a list, the *Venosta* was stopped in her tracks. It was all too apparent to Captain Myhre that more than a school of fish had come into the mouth of his net. His position at the time was 43° 24′ north and 61° 27′30″ west and the drag was in 40 fathoms of water. Captain Myhre gave the order to haul back and see if the net would come free. The great steam winches, straining their utmost, slowly began to wind in the heavy cables, bringing with them whatever it was they had snagged. Slowly, ever so slowly, the cables came aboard, when suddenly, there in the moonlight beside the *Venosta*, appeared a set of mastheads which rose majestically higher and higher. Still the cables came in and still this spectre from the deep, snatched so rudely from its grave, rose ever higher. Though devoid of topmasts and sails, the lower sticks stood proudly erect, the standing rigging still essentially intact. Shortly the hull itself, on a perfectly even keel, broke from the calm depths to the surface of a turbulent sea to survey again the elements in which she had lived and died.

Aboard the *Venosta* there was a dead silence, the crew utterly mesmerized by the spectacle they were witnessing. They rubbed their eyes in utter amazement at what seemed to be this supernatural appearance of a phantom ship in the moonlit waters beside them. For moments they stood, rooted to the deck. Suddenly, as the full realization of the event took them, they moved into action, determined to find out the realities of their dubious prize. Captain Myhre ordered all floodlights turned on and directed towards the derelict. The brilliant electric glare revealed a beautiful schooner in a remarkable state of preservation. Her lower masts still stood, held by shrouds largely undamaged. Though gaffs, booms, and bowsprit were gone, the hull was perfectly preserved and showed little marine growth. Even the paint looked fresh. From a distance she might, for all intents and purposes, have been a schooner lying at anchor for the night. As the bright lights moved over the deck, they struck the forecastle companionway. Again a hush fell over *Venosta*'s crew as in their imaginations they peopled the ghostly blackness of that opening with the forms of those who must have been imprisoned there. With the drama of this ghostly visit unfolding before their eyes, the horrible realization dawned on Captain Myhre and his men that they had resurrected the *Columbia*. There was no question in their minds. It could be no other. Her name, to be sure, could not be made out, but the many who remembered her well were certain it was she.

The somewhat trance-like contemplation of their captive by *Venosta*'s men was shortly to be broken by the practical realities of the situation. A fairly good sea was running and the two vessels were beginning to slam together, threatening to batter the sides of the *Venosta*. Captain Myhre would have to do something and do it soon. But at that point the problem was solved for him; the cables parted under the strain and the load was released, taking the net and trawl gear with it. As she had risen from the

162

depths, so now did the schooner sink back again. For a few short minutes she had ridden again upon the waves, seen the moonlight, felt the wind in her rigging—a sentient thing vibrant with a life briefly renewed. Now she sank resignedly to the grave from which she had come. In a sudden swirl of white water she was gone.

As he came ashore in Halifax, Captain Myhre, trembling with emotion, told of his experience. "I can never describe how we felt," he exclaimed. "She was a phantom ship and she came up beside us, and as slowly as she emerged from the water on a perfectly even keel, so did she go back again to the deep."

Appendixes

Sail plan of the *Columbia*. Drawing by Edward S. Bosley

COMPARATIVE MEASUREMENTS

Schooner	Bluenose	Columbia	Henry Ford	Puritan	Mayflower	Elsie
Designer	Wm. J. Roué	W. Starling Burgess	Thomas F. McManus	W. Starling Burgess	W. Starling Burgess	Thomas F. McManus
Builder	Smith & Rhuland, Lunenburg, N.S.	Arthur D. Story Essex, Mass.	Arthur D. Story Essex, Mass.	Everett B. James Essex, Mass.	Everett B. James Essex, Mass.	Arthur D. Story Essex, Mass.
Date launched	Mar. 26, 1921	Apr. 17, 1923	Apr. 11, 1922	Mar. 15, 1922	Apr. 12, 1921	May 9, 1910
Overall length	143	141-3	139	139	143-7	124
Length on waterline	112	110	109	106	112	102.6
Registered length	130.2	123.9	122.1	123.9	131.6	106.5
Breadth	27	25.8	26	25.7	25.9	25
Depth	13	12.4	12	11.8	12	11.5
Draft	15-10	15-8	15-7	15-5½	16	14-6
Gross tons	153	152.67	155	149	164	137
Net tons	99	96	90	96	113	98
Mainmast: *deck to cap	96	93 (7' lap)	100	89*	91*	76*
Foremast: *deck to cap	83	83 (6' lap)	87	77*	78-6*	68*
Main topmast	48	48-6	52	51	52	45
Fore topmast	45	43-6	44	45	42	43
Main boom	81-6	78-4	76	75-7	72	75
Fore boom	32-10	32-4	32	31	34-6	29-6
Main gaff	51	49	46	46	44-6	44
Fore gaff	32-11	32	32	31	34-6	
Sail area (allowed)	10,035.2	9,680	9,504.8	8,988.8	10,035.2	8,421.4
Sail area (designed)	10,901	10,220			10,785	
Displacement, long tons	280	264				
Projection of bowsprit	17-6	17	abt. 17	15-6		25-8

BILL OF MATERIALS AND EXPENDITURES
FOR A CHALLENGER

The following tables were compiled by John M. Clayton in the course of his extensive research into the records of Essex shipbuilding.

EXPENDITURES FOR COLUMBIA

Excerpted from the checkbook of A. D. Story. There were obviously many more expenditures, but only these were specifically marked for *Columbia*.

1922

Nov. 29	Bliss Bros: Misc. hardware	$ 176.50
Dec. 28	Dodge-Haley Co.: 2 kegs (400 lbs.) 4 × 5/16"; 2 kegs 4½ × 5/16"; 1 keg 5 × 5/16"; 5 kegs 5 × 3/8"; 2 kegs 6 × 3/8" galvanized ship spikes	216.50

1923

Jan. 31	Olin S. Ellis: U. S. Lloyd's on Sch. *Columbia*, $18,000	225.00
Feb. 23	Boston-Lockport Block Co.:	
	4 5½" lignum vitae deadeyes	7.00
	16 7" ditto	44.00
Mar. 23	J. W. Aulson & Sons:	
	1 set of 10" rudder braces	54.08
	1 brass hawse pipe	15.00
Apr. 17	Thales Cook: piloting to Gloucester	20.00
Apr. 28	Finlayson & Jenkins: carving, gilding, painting boards, pipes, name and Hail (bow & stern)	38.00
Apr. –	George E. Thurston: set of spars	1,300.00
May 1	Edwin C. Perkins: to 59 days' labor on *Columbia* at $6 per day	354.00
May 17	John M. Closson: painting out cabin and forecastle and supplying materials	162.45
May –	Charles A. Marr:	
	4445 lbs. of Hull ironwork at 19¢	844.55
	large buffer	72.00
	second buffer	65.00
	20" windlass	70.00
	45 lbs. 3/4 × 5/8 bolts at 8¢	3.60
	12 rings	.15
	teaming	1.00

These and the following tables are for the schooner *Puritan* and approximate closely the expenditures for *Columbia*.

	used	bought	charge	unit	credit	charge
Keel, shoe & deadwood	3,090	—	3,090	$ .90		$ 278.10
Sternpost, stem & knees	883	—	883	.65		57.39
Knees	130	125	5	3.00		15.00
Beams, carlings, frame timbers, etc.	30,902	16,993	13,969	.50		698.45
Hard pine plank	18,833	9,151	9,682	.66		639.01
Outside & ceiling	4,322	3,096	1,226	.79		96.85
Oak plank	10,470		10,470	.90		942.30
2" pine planksheer, 4" pine & W.P. decking	2,231	—	2,231	.65		145.01
Oregon deck	7,150	—	7,150	.75		536.25
7/8" Pine boards	3,000	—	3,000	.65		195.00
Iron	187.82	202.81			15.00	
Spikes	99.00	99.00				
Treenails	13,000	—	13,000	.01		130.00
White paint	6 gal.	10 gal.	4 gal.	2.70	10.80	

$25.80 $3,733.36
charge: $3,707.56

*Lumber prices per 1,000 bd. ft.; some items from yard stock.

COSTS

1921

Nov.	25	Payroll	$ 44.60
Dec.	2	Ditto	153.50
	3	Freight on iron	33.40
	9	Payroll	345.05
	10	Glou. Elec. Co.: Power, mo. of Nov.	11.59
	15	P. S. Huckins Co.: Hard pine	390.51
	16	Payroll	349.16
	16	Dodge-Haley Co.: Iron	202.82
	21	P. S. Huckins Co.: Hard pine	242.13
	23	Payroll	290.41
	30	Ditto	270.59
	28	B & M R.R.: Freight on Janvrin timber	75.87

1922

Jan.	2	Payroll	425.95
	3	Chase & Janvrin: On a/c 6,933′ timber	150.00
	10	Glou. Elec. Co.: Power, mo. of Dec. 1921	31.86
	13	Payroll	443.53
	14	Chase & Janvrin: Bal. a/c timber	122.99
	14	P. S. Huckins Co.: Hard pine	198.38
	16	B & M R.R.: Freight on knees	51.50
	16	A. L. Young: Bal. on 125-5″ hackmatack knee	317.03
	18	S. Knight & Sons Co.: Cement	15.40
	18	Dodge-Haley Co.: Spikes	99.00
	20	Payroll	597.24
	27	Ditto	268.70
	30	B & M R.R.: Freight on 2 boxes of paint	.50
	30	Holt & Bugbee Co.: Dry lumber, finish	352.10
	31	A. W. Eaton: Teaming in Dec. & Jan.	46.10
Feb.	3	Sherwin-Williams Co.: White paint	26.98
	3	W. A. Gates: Millwork on timber	9.00
	3	Payroll	573.13
	11	C. L. Knowlton: 3 loads gravel for cement	10.50
	11	Taunton-Bedford Cop. Co.: Copper sheet & rod	5.96
	11	Glou. Elec. Co.: Power, mo. of Jan.	39.34
	11	Payroll	539.07
	18	Ditto	324.93
	20	B & M R.R.: Freight on pumps & pipe	1.49
	25	Payroll	327.98

Mar.	1	Am. Ex. Co.: Express on rudder braces	2.95
	2	A. W. Eaton: Ex. & teaming, mo. of Feb.	32.00
	4	L. E. Perkins: Nails	.40
	4	Payroll	383.70
	10	Isaac Brown: 10,000 ft. timber	500.00
	10	Glou. Elec. Co.: mo. of Feb.	16.54
	10	Hub Galv. Works: Galvanizing	131.92
	11	Payroll	577.33
	13	Am. Ex. Co.: Express	.60
	13	L. E. Perkins: Nails, etc.	5.20
	18	J. Finlayson: Carving & Gilding	40.00
	18	Payroll	489.48
	18	Thales Cook: Pilot Fee	35.00
	24	Am. Ex. Co.: Box from Bliss Bros.	.45
	24	Bus fare; O. O. Story & C. Mulcahy	2.75
	25	Payroll	110.75
	25	Glidden Co.: Whiting, spirits & brushes	20.68
Apr.	3	A. P. Stoddart Co.: Steerer	120.00
	3	Geo. A. Reed & Son: Hawse pipe, chocks and windlass	105.45
	3	J. W. Aulson & Sons: Rudder braces	84.58
	3	Albert Russell's Sons: Pumps & pipe	56.71
	3	A. B. Poland: Molds, posts & make windlass	184.70
	3	O. O. Story: Making bolts & other ironwork	53.80
	3	Master Mariners Towboat Co.: Towing	85.00
	3	A. S. Morss: Hardware	35.51
	3	Bliss Bros.: Cotton, nails, portlights	210.75
	3	George H. Pierce: Ironwork	50.25
	3	Launching grease	10.00
	3	Yard rent 4 mos. at $6.25	25.00
		Use of Horse: 102 days at $1	102.00
		Use of mill beside the power, 102 days at $1	102.00
		Bus fares: Mal. MacIver & M. Cogswell	4.00
		Timber and other material more than is accounted for in above statement	3,707.56
		Workmen's compensation ins. on payroll of $5,914.87 at 2.403	158.99
		A. W. Eaton: Express, mo. of March	7.95
		Hub. Galv. Works: Bill of Apr. 1, 1922	57.20
		John M. Closson, painting cabin & f'castle	103.80
			$15,003.29
		E. B. James, 10% commission on above	1,500.32
			$16,503.61

Spars	1,375.00
Iron work	850.00
Oakum	162.00
	$18,890.61

PAYMENTS

1921-1922

Nov.	21	1st payment, Benj. Pine & others	$ 700.00
Dec.	13	2nd payment, "The Manta Club"	1,000.00
	17	3rd ditto	1,000.00
	31	4th ditto	1,000.00
Jan.	14	5th ditto	2,000.00
Feb.	3	6th ditto	2,000.00
Mar.	4	7th ditto	2,000.00
Apr.	6	8th ditto	2,300.00
May	20	9th ditto	1,000.00
Oct.	3	10th & final payment	3,003.29
		Discount	500.00
			$16,503.29

WORKERS

The following men worked on the *Columbia* or in the A. D. Story Yard during the period from December 16, 1922, through April 1923. An asterisk denotes those who worked the full period.

Leonard Amero
Willard Andrews*
William Atkins
Alan Brewton
Stanwood Burnham*
John Coffill
Liboire D'Entremont*
Leandre Doucette
John Doyle
John J. Doyle*
George P. Gray*
John Hubbard*
Mark Hubbard
Peter Hubbard
Thomas Irving

Malcolm MacIver*
John Murphy*
Arthur Norton*
Edwin C. Perkins
William Ross
Edwin J. Story*
Frank W. Story*
George G. Story*
Jacob Story*
Harry Swett*
"L.J.S."
Fred Watson
George Weston*
"Leo"

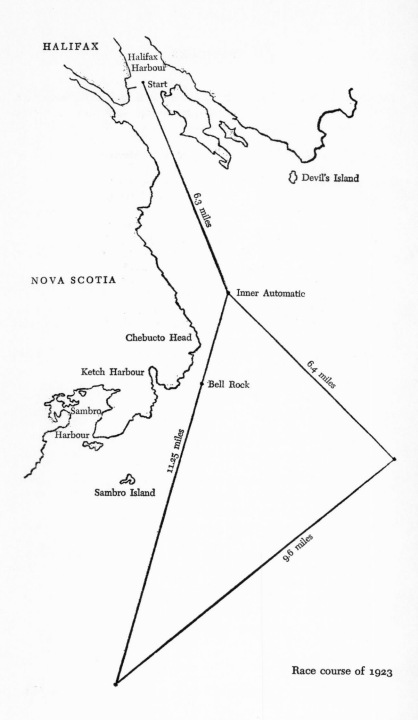

HALIFAX

Halifax
Harbour

Start

Devil's Island

6.3 miles

NOVA SCOTIA

Inner Automatic

Chebucto Head

6.4 miles

Ketch Harbour

Bell Rock

Sambro

Harbour

11.25 miles

Sambro Island

9.6 miles

Race course of 1923

Bibliography

Backman, Brian and Phil. *Bluenose*. Toronto: McClelland and Stewart, 1965.

Church, Albert Cook, and Connolly, James B. *American Fishermen*. New York: W. W. Norton & Co., 1940.

Connolly, James B. *The Book of the Gloucester Fishermen*. New York: The John Day Co., 1927.

Connolly, James B. *The Port of Gloucester*. New York: Doubleday, Doran and Co., 1940.

Information Kit—Bluenose II. Halifax: Profile Ltd.

Memorial of the Celebration of the 250th Anniversary of the Incorporation of the Town of Gloucester, Mass. Gloucester: City of Gloucester, 1901.

New England Fishing Schooners, Ships & Sailing Album #4. Milwaukee: Kalmback Publishing Co., 1947.

Pierce, Wesley George. *Goin' Fishin'*. Salem: Marine Research Society, 1934.

Pigeon, Fred. "The Mayflower Story." *The National Fisherman*, April 1969, pp. 145-158.

Thomas, Gordon W. *Fast and Able*. Gloucester: Historic Ships Associates, 1968.

PRIMARY SOURCES

Annual listings of the merchant vessels of the United States, published by the U.S. Government

Annual reports of the Town of Essex.

Detailed plans and drawings of *Columbia* by Edward Sohier Bosley, Scarsdale, N.Y.

Files of the *Atlantic Fisherman* (Goffstown, N.H.), *Boston Evening Transcript, Boston Globe, Boston Herald, Boston Post, Gloucester Daily Times, New York Times, Salem Evening News*.

Miscellaneous records and papers from the collection of Lewis H. Story, Essex, Mass.

Records of the Story Shipyard and James Shipyard compiled by John M. Clayton, Rockport, Mass. (Part of these appeared in *American Neptune* ix, January 1940, pp. 73-74.)

Time book of the Arthur D. Story Shipyard, 1922-1930.

Yearbooks of the Fishermen's Union of the Atlantic.

Yearbooks of the Gloucester Master Mariners' Association.